surface of the brick with a wire brush.

The correct mortar mix should be used when re-pointing and as a small amount will go a long way it is adviseable to purchase a proprietary ready-mixed bag such as Marley Mix. Water is then added as required.

Match up to the existing mortar joint which will usually be a rubbed, flush or weathered joint.

If a large amount of mortar is needed, make it by mixing Portland cement, fine sand and some pva adhesive (plasticiser) – and water. The mix must be neither too stiff nor too runny. A 'buttery' consistency is best. Follow manufacturer's instructions when using pva adhesive.

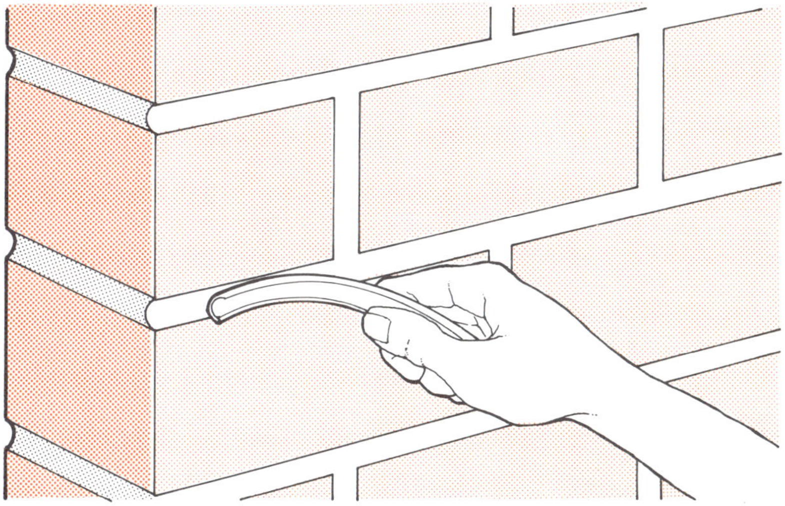

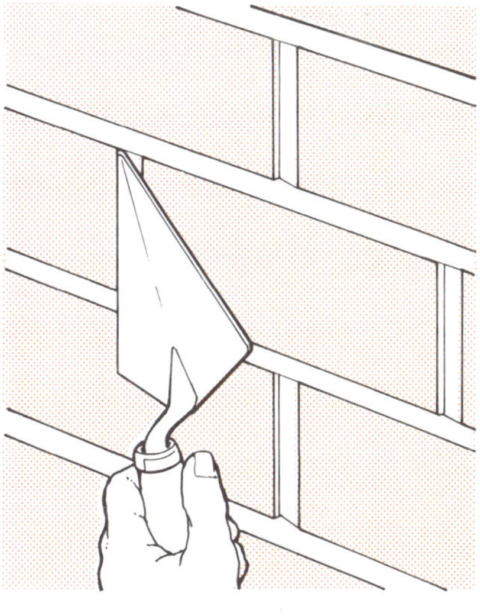

Use a small sharp cold chisel and club hammer to chip out the old mortar to a depth of $\frac{3}{4}$in. Brush out all dust and soak the cavity with water. Wetting first prevents the bricks from absorbing too much moisture from the mortar.

Use a trowel to press the mortar into the cavities. Leave the mortar slightly proud of the surface.

When the mortar is partially dry, rub off the excess. Use a half round length of timber or a short length of pipe.

Use the edge of the trowel to shape the horizontal joints. The mortar must slope outwards to the bottom edge.

Weathered pointing is more difficult to master. Complete the vertical joints by drawing the trowel back towards the right-hand bricks while pressing inwards with the left side of the trowel. Use the edge of the trowel to slice surplus mortar off the face of the bricks.

Damaged bricks A single damaged brick can be removed and replaced quite easily. If the wall is to be painted it is not important to buy a matching brick. If it is not being painted, then see if a builders' merchant can supply a used brick of the same type.

The space (usually 2in.) between the outer and inner leaf of a cavity wall prevents rainwater reaching the inside wall of the house and causing damp problems. If any of the pieces of brick being removed drop into and become lodged in the cavity they will form a bridge for rainwater to cross to the inside wall. So be careful when chipping out a brick. Make sure that the line of mortar around the four sides of the hole are also chipped clean, so that fresh mortar can be pressed around the replacement brick.

When chipping out a brick from a solid wall, use a small, sharp cold chisel to clean out the brick and surrounding mortar. If a club hammer and larger brick bolster are used, it is all too easy to damage the internal brick and for the plaster to be cracked and dislodged from the inner wall.

Use a cold chisel and club hammer to chip away the damaged brick. Work from the centre outwards. It is very important to use a small sharp cold chisel and take out only small pieces of the brick at a time to avoid internal damage in a solid brick wall.

'Butter' mortar around the new brick and slide it into the cavity. Tap the brick into its final position by using the handle of the trowel. Take care not to push the brick too far into a cavity wall as it will be difficult to extract. Complete the pointing as before.

A continuous crack down a wall can indicate a major fault in the foundations. Get qualified help as repairs will certainly have to be carried out by a professional builder.

ALL ABOUT HOUSE REPAIR AND MAINTENANCE

ROY DAY

HAMLYN
London · New York · Sydney · Toronto

Contents

The illustrations on pages 110 and 111 are reproduced by courtesy of THE RAWLPLUG COMPANY LIMITED

Published by
The Hamlyn Publishing Group Ltd
Astronaut House, Feltham, Middlesex, England
London · New York · Sydney · Toronto

ISBN 0 600 30300 4
Printed in England by Chapel River Press (IPC Printers) Ltd

Introduction

The days of the ubiquitous odd-job man are rapidly becoming a thing of the past. Home maintenance is no longer catered for by a quick telephone call to that 'little man around the corner' who will effect a speedy and economical repair. And everything from a leaking tap or a blocked drain to a loose roof tile or a broken window was within his repertoire.

Times have changed. Labour charges have escalated along with everything else and nowadays most homeowners have to fend for themselves.

This book has been written for those people who are forced through economy to tackle a variety of smaller jobs themselves to keep their house in good running order. It does not, and is not intended to, cover major jobs that require a good deal of practical experience and know-how.

Major repair work, thankfully, is not a regular requirement. However, there are a host of other jobs that crop up from time to time that can be tackled successfully with a minimum amount of practical ability – provided that the information about repair materials, tools and techniques is available in a simple, straightforward form. That information is given in this book. By tackling all the jobs described, the homeowner will build up a store of experience and technique to the point where he will never again have to wait for professional help for routine repairs.

Maintaining a house and garden is essential if the houseowner is to protect his investment. The best approach is to keep maintenance going as a routine. This way a sudden work load, where everything has gone wrong at once, will be avoided. Keep a diary of things to do each week, each month or each year. This way the house will never get on top of you. Carry out a regular inspection as a sure way of anticipating problems before they get worse or result in expensive damage.

With materials costing so much, advance planning is important if half-full packets or boxes of repair materials are not to be wasted. If they are left over, then some of the cost of doing it yourself will be wasted. So if you buy materials for one job, try to find in advance good uses for left-overs in case you buy too much.

Looking After Walls

BRICKWORK

Efflorescence – a white powdery substance that forms on brickwork – is caused by water drawing the soluble salts in the bricks to the surface.

Since water causes the trouble, do not attempt to wash away the substance; this will add to the problem.

Using an old distemper brush, apply a fluid called 'Efforless' which will neutralise the soluble salts. Usually three coats are needed and this type of fluid is readily available at most builders' merchants. Should difficulty be experienced in obtaining a supply, contact any leading paint manufacturer to find a local stockist.

Damp walls may give rise to vegetation or fungus growth. Here, use a stiff broom (not a wire brush) to clean down the wall before brushing on a coat of fungicide. The cause of the damp (see p. 18) must be cured or the trouble will reoccur.

Efflorescence and fungus growth can appear on interior walls and spoil wallpaper. In this case, there is no alternative but to strip off the paper, complete the remedial work and then redecorate. As an added precaution use a wallpaper paste containing a fungicide.

Often solid brick walls which face the prevailing winds can be saturated by driving rain, which can cause efflorescence. A liberal application of silicone solution to the brickwork in dry summer conditions will prevent rain soaking into the bricks.

Rust can occur in the mortar joints between the bricks. One of the ingredients used to make mortar is sand. The rust is caused by ironstone present in the sand. Chip out the old mortar and fill the joints with freshly mixed mortar.

Repointing If the mortar joints have started to crumble or crack, the whole wall will soon look shabby. Even sound, discoloured joints can ruin the appearance of attractive brickwork. In both cases it is worthwhile raking out the old mortar and filling the joints with new.

If any mortar drops on to the face of the bricks, do not try to clean it off immediately; you will only succeed in spreading it further over the surface. Allow it to dry and then scrape it off with a trowel. Then lightly brush the

There are three types of joint. Make sure you repoint (make good) defective joints to match those used previously. Flush joints are the most common. These leave a flat surface. They should be used where a wall is to be painted.

Weathered joints are slanted to make sure rainwater slides off, thus preventing it settling and sinking into the mortar. Rubbed joints are formed with a half round length of metal or timber.

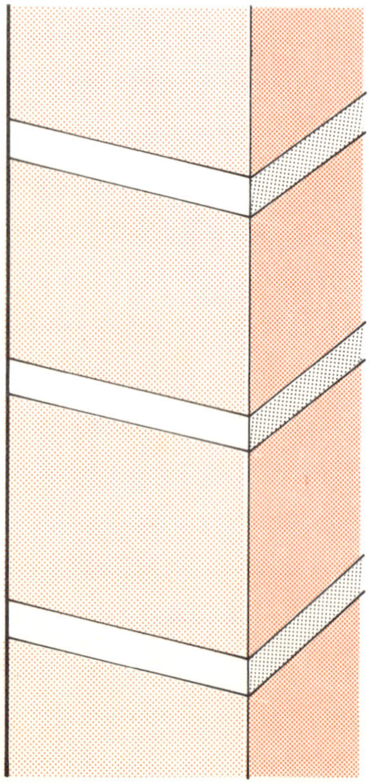

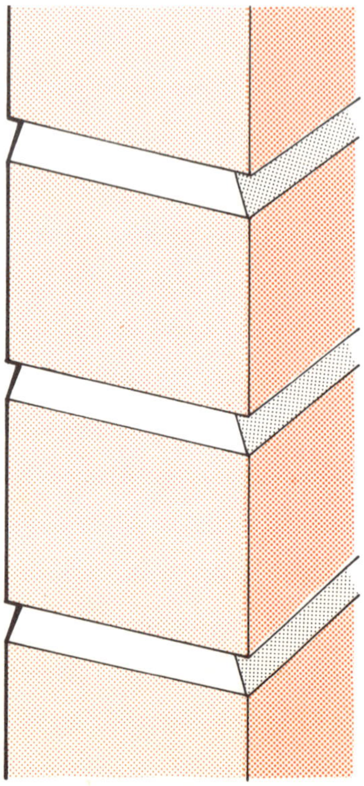

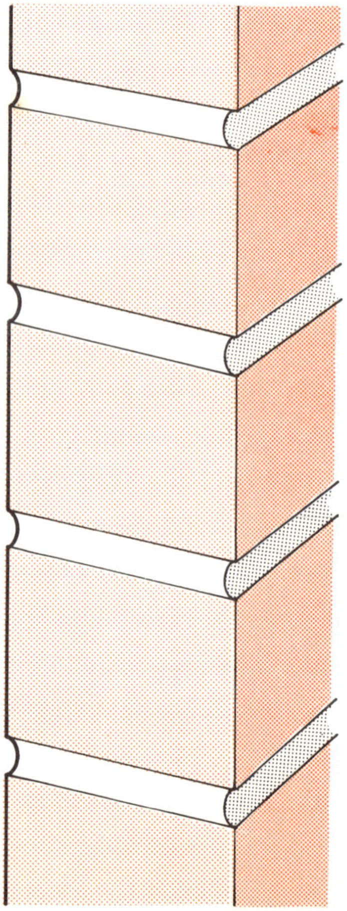

Replacing an airbrick The grid formation of an airbrick allows fresh air to pass through the walls but prevents birds or vermin getting inside. If it is damaged it must be replaced immediately.

There are two types of airbrick. The type for a solid wall comprises a brick and louvre which are fixed to the outside and inside of the wall respectively. A cavity wall airbrick extends right through the wall.

Knock out the damaged airbrick using a cold chisel and club hammer. Work from the centre outwards. Remember to see that all airbricks around the house are above path level and not blocked up by soil or any other obstruction piled against them. Blocked vents will prevent the air circulating and can cause wet rot in the ground floor joists and floorboards.

Spread a ½in. layer of mortar on the base of the hole and a similar thickness around the new airbrick.

Push the brick into the hole and make good the pointing to match the surrounding area.

RENDERING REPAIRS

The rendering over the brickwork of a house wall (on solid walls) prevents rainwater reaching the bricks of the outer face of the wall and thereafter crossing to the inner walls to cause damp patches which ruin decorations.

Should a damp patch appear, check the outside wall to see if the rendering is cracked or damaged. Sometimes defects are not immediately apparent; gentle tapping along a suspect area with a hammer will find defective patches – they will sound hollow and could fall out even under a light tap. For repairs, use a mortar mix of 1 part Portland cement to 6 parts sand. The sand should be a mixture of soft and sharp sand.

For smaller cracks use a proprietary mix, available from d-i-y shops in small bags.

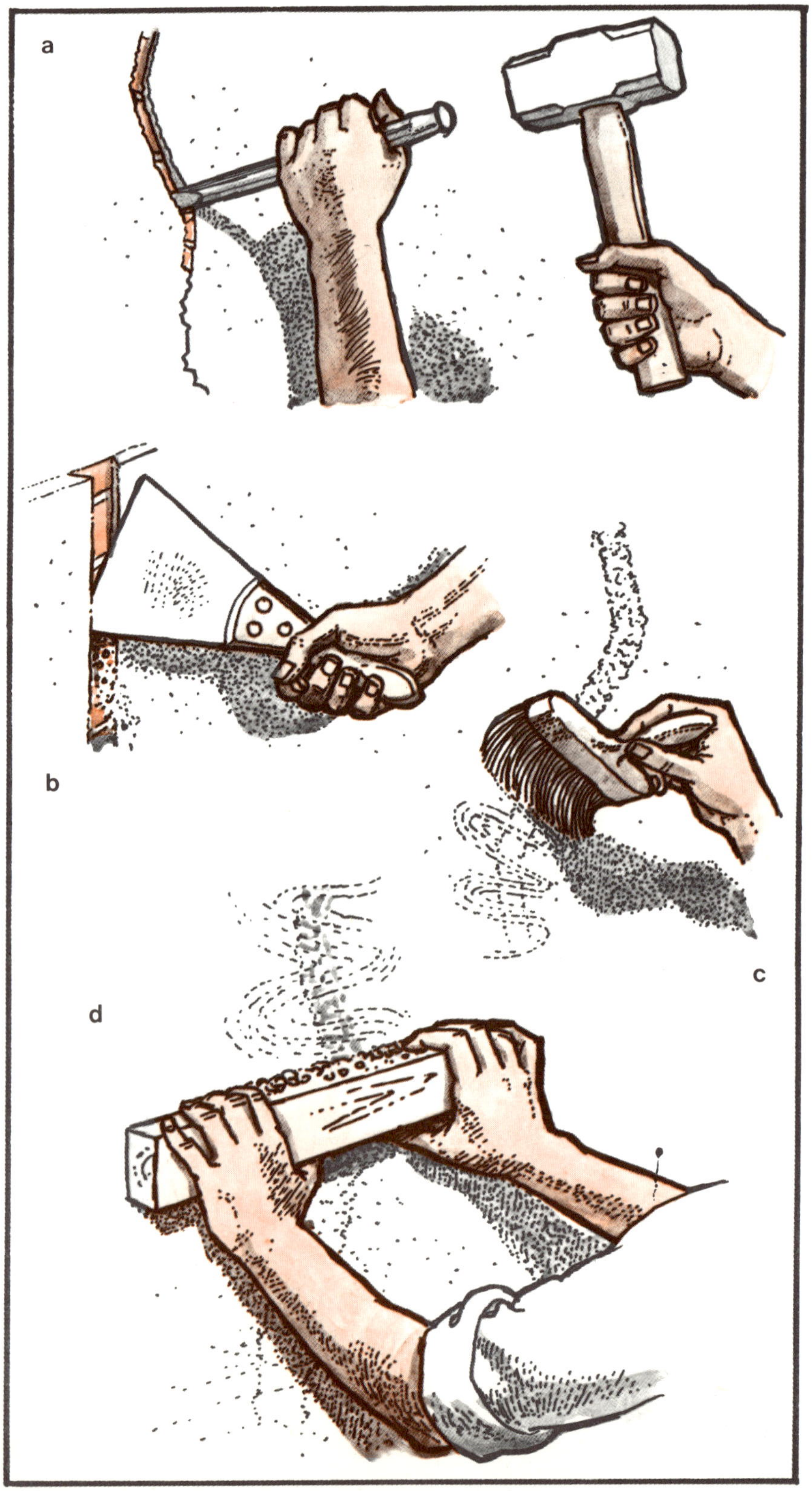

Use a sharp cold chisel and club hammer to widen the crack. (a)

Undercut the edges with a scraper so that the new mortar can be pressed behind the crack. Remove all loose material using a wire brush. Brush a pva bonding agent, proprietary type, into the crack. (b)

Press the mortar well into the crack using a scraper. Remove excess mortar immediately, using an old damp brush. (c)

Allow the mortar to dry partially before damping down and smoothing off with a trowel or a block of wood. (d)

PEBBLEDASH

An 'invisible' repair can be made to an area of damaged pebbledash by adding some pebbles to mortar spread over the damaged area before painting.

Use a mortar mix of 1 part Portland cement and 6 parts sand. Try to buy pebbles from a builder's merchant as near as possible in size to the existing pebbles.

Cut back all damaged pebbles and mortar to leave sound edges around the damage. If necessary, chip back to brickwork using a broad cold chisel. (a)

Trowel mortar into the cavity, level off and, while it is still wet, throw on the pebbles. (b)

Press the pebbles well into the mortar using a wood float. (c)

When the mortar is dry, use a large worn brush to punch paint well into the wall surface. Gloss paint provides an easy-to-clean finish and helps to make the repair invisible. (d)

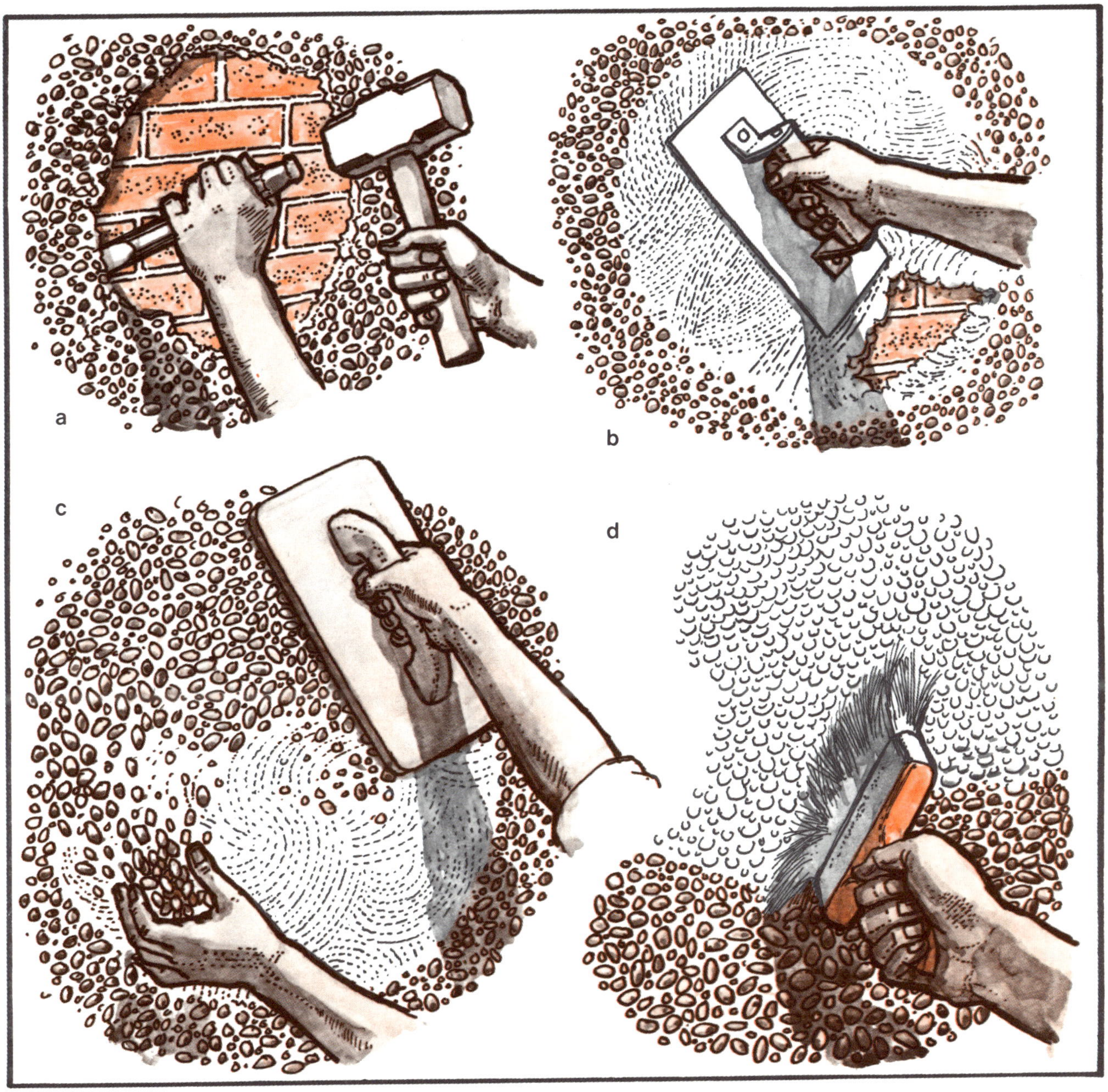

CRACKS IN CEILINGS AND WALLS

The method of repairing holes and cracks in ceilings and interior walls depends on the extent of the damage and the situation.

Smaller cracks can usually be repaired with a cellulose filler whereas large cracks in ceilings will need different treatment.

Wide cracks Wide ceiling cracks or those which re-open after filling indicate excessive ceiling movement. This is a common problem. If you fill these cracks with a cellulose filler you will probably be back to square one in no time.

However, it may be possible to achieve a permanent, invisible repair by using a scrim mesh and, if necessary, lining paper.

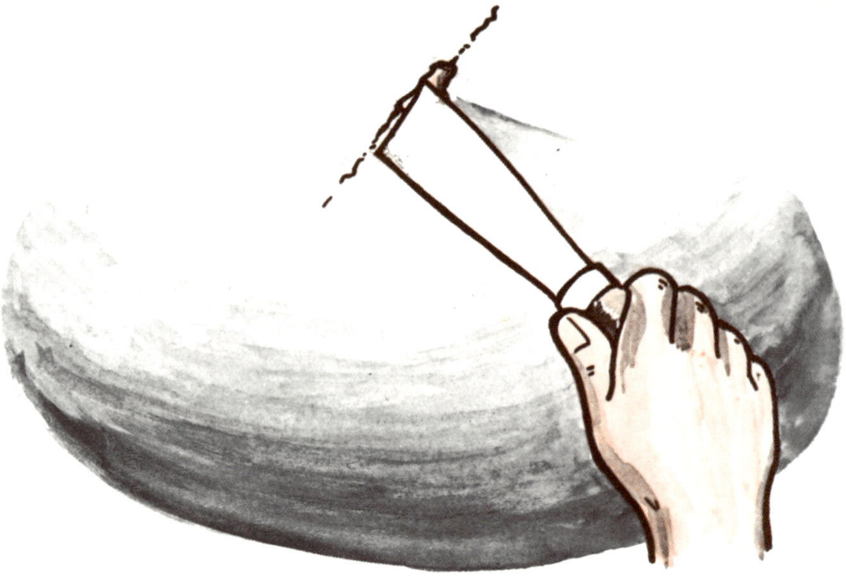

Whether in ceilings or walls, fill all nail holes and smaller cracks with cellulose filler such as Polyfilla. Before filling a crack you must first undercut it with a filling knife. Undercutting means deepening the cavity behind the crack to form a V-shape. The V should be widest at its deepest part.

Dust all loose material from the crack and fill the cavity with the filler. Allow to set before rubbing flush with the surface using glasspaper wrapped around a wood block. A flush finish can also be achieved by drawing the filling knife at right angles across the surface. A 3in. filling knife with a flexible blade is ideal.

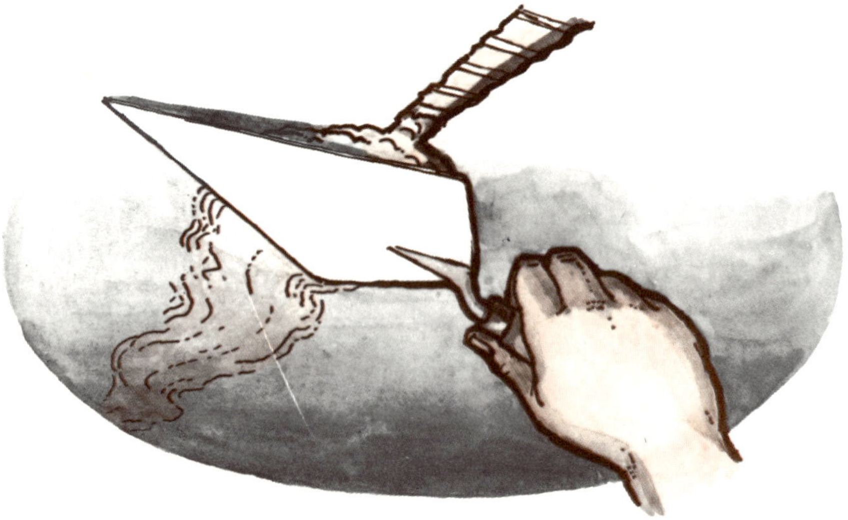

For large areas it is more economical to use a plaster such as Sirapite. Dampen the crack beforehand and apply the plaster with a trowel. Sirapite sets quickly so work in a continuous session.

To get a flush finish, draw a timber straight-edge across the wet plaster to level it off. Rub a steel float across the area when the plaster is touch dry. This will leave a smooth surface.

If you prefer, fill the bulk of the cavity with plaster. Allow to dry and then 'top up' with cellulose filler, as before, using a filling knife.

Alternatively fill the crack with cellulose filler. Cut out some scrim mesh (available from decorating shops; it is sold in rolls) and stick it over the crack with cellulose paste. The scrim should be slightly longer than the crack. (a)

When dry, cover the mesh with filler. Allow this to set and then rub it smooth with the surface. (b)

To add more strength to the repair, tear off a piece of lining paper about 1ft wide. Paste the central 6in. with cellulose paste and brush it over the repaired area leaving its 'dry' border hanging down. (c)

When dry, tear off the border to leave a feathered edge on the ceiling. To completely disguise the feathered edge, apply a thin coat of cellulose filler, having first primed the surface with emulsion paint. (d)

Fix a timber straight-edge to an external corner as a guide when repairing with thistle plaster.

Loose plaster Chimney breasts and other areas near fireplaces are likely points at which to find whole chunks of loose plaster. These should be lifted out with a broad knife, if necessary going right back to the brickwork. Repairs can then be made with Sirapite.

When repairing an external corner of a window or doorway, use thistle plaster. This dries rock hard and will stand knocks.

Any plaster of this type which is left too long before use will start to harden in the container. Do not add fresh water to the mix to activate it or it will set hard immediately. So always use fresh material.

Plastering electric cable channels
Before working in the vicinity of electrical wires, always turn off the current at the mains.

The wiring from a wall switch should be covered with protective plastic conduit before plastering with Sirapite. These conduits should always be used when cable is to be fed into walls and covered with plaster.

It will be necessary to unscrew the switch cover in order to plaster around the switch box sunk in the wall.

Fixing decorative coverings
Laminate This is bought in large sheets, about $\frac{1}{16}$in. thick, and cut down to the required size. A variety of colours is available. The surface of

Fit plastic conduit over wires and brush out all dust from the cavity.

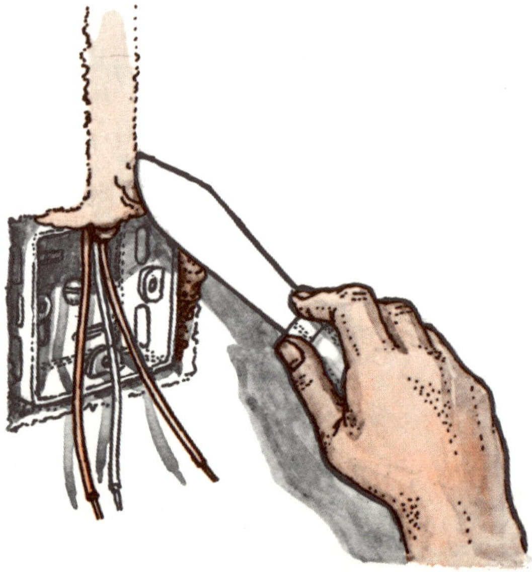

Dampen the cavity with fresh water before plastering. Make sure that the plaster is well packed around the switch box and the plastic conduit. Allow the plaster to dry before refixing the switch cover. All power should be switched off when undertaking this type of repair.

laminate will resist all normal domestic stains.

It is simple to cut, using a Stanley knife fitted with a special laminate blade. Alternatively, a fine-tooth handsaw can be used. Cut the laminate about $\frac{1}{8}$in. oversize. Trim off this surplus edge when the piece is glued firmly in place.

Adhesive is used to fix the laminate. Contact adhesive can be used though here you must get the positioning absolutely right first time since the laminate will stick firmly immediately it touches the surface. A water-based resin adhesive such as Cascamite does allow time for the laminate to be repositioned, but it must be clamped while drying.

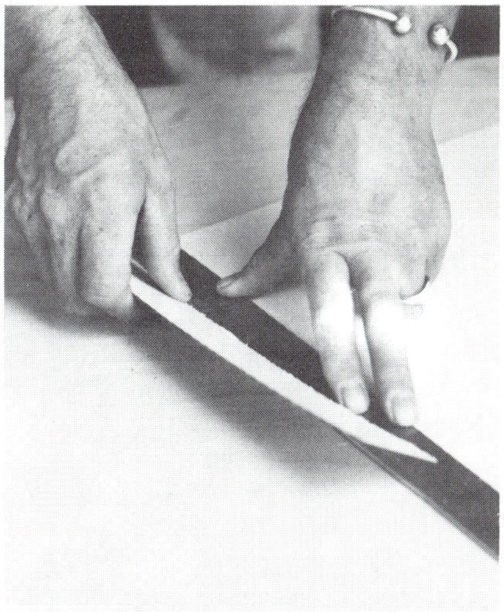

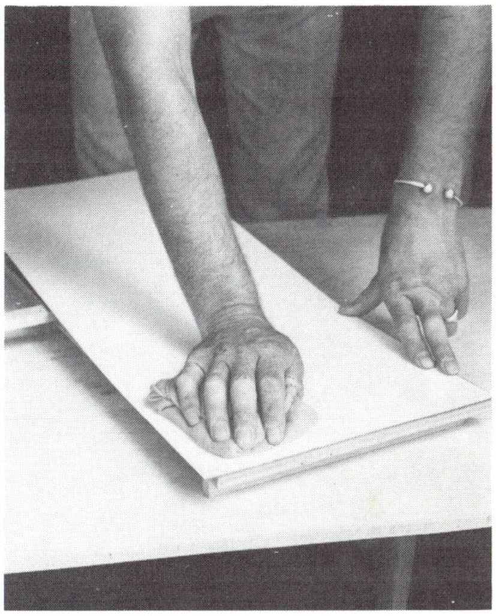

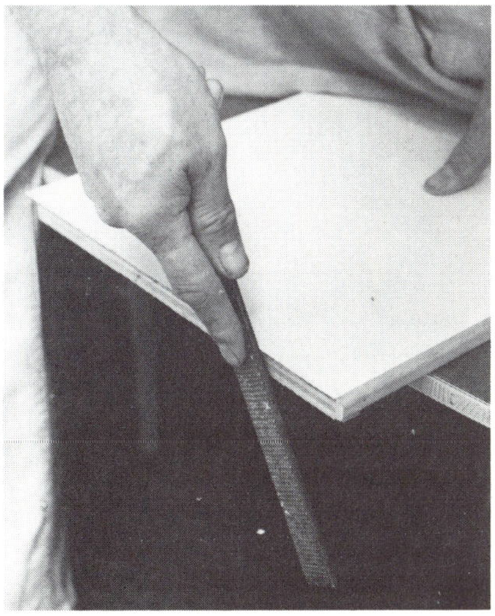

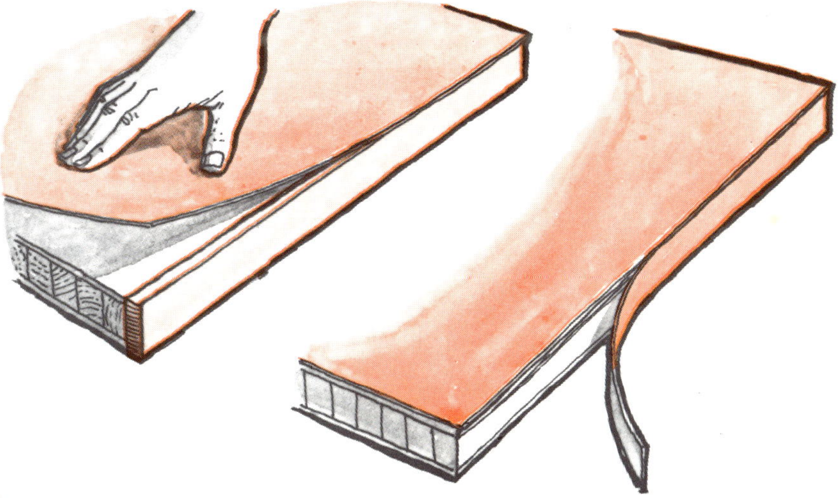

To cut laminate, lay it on a flat surface. Score along the decorative face with a laminate blade held against a straight-edge. Continue scoring until the sheet is cut at least halfway through.
Holding the straight-edge firmly down, fold the waste side upwards, to break the laminate cleanly. If preferred, the sheet can be cut right through without the need to snap along the line.

If using contact adhesive, place battens on the surface and position the laminate over them. Gradually remove battens, working from one end, and press the sheet into place. This is a useful method of getting the positioning right first time. Finish off by sliding a smooth block of wood over the surface and tapping firmly with a hammer to form a firm bond between laminate and the core board.

If pva or a resin-based adhesive is used, the sheet will have to be clamped in position until the glue has set.

Trim off the surplus $\frac{1}{8}$in. with a sharp block plane. Alternatively, use a fine file.

Edges can be lipped with offcuts or with a special edging strip obtainable at d-i-y shops. It is advisable, wherever possible, to fix the edging strip first.

Mirror tiles Mirror tiles are sold in a whole range of sizes so you can plan each area so as to avoid having to cut any tiles.

These tiles are not precision made so widths and lengths of 'same-size' tiles can vary slightly. It is best to lay out the tiles 'dry' to ascertain the best arrangement. Number each tile on the surface and indicate its position, using a grease pencil or lipstick.

Other coverings Self-adhesive flexible coverings such as Fablon are simple to cut and fit. A wide choice of patterns and designs is available. These coverings must be fixed to a dry, clean, smooth surface.

Each tile has four adhesive pads on the back covered by a protective paper. This is stripped off and the tile pressed firmly into place. The positioning must be right first time since, once they touch the surface, they are well stuck down.

If covering a door, to avoid cutting any tiles the door can be framed with plywood, covered with laminate. Build the frame up to leave a flush surface with the tiles.

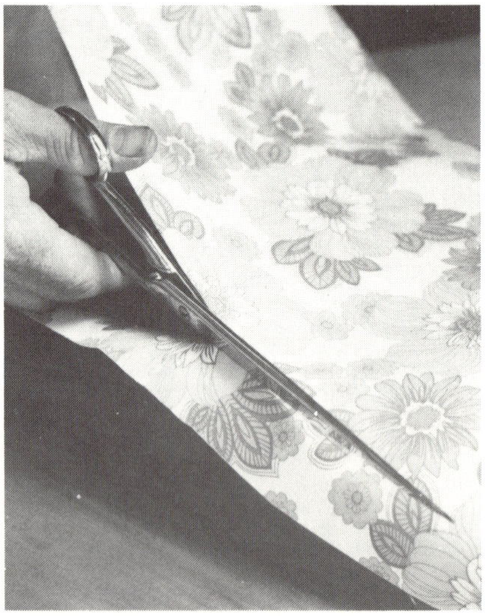

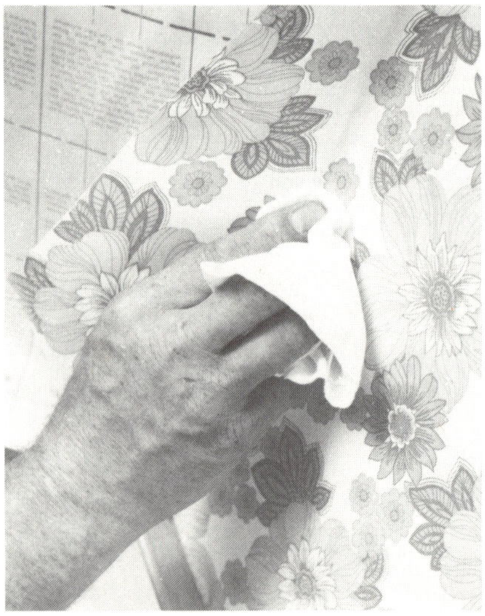

Cut Fablon to size with scissors.

Smooth it in place on the surface, avoiding wrinkles.

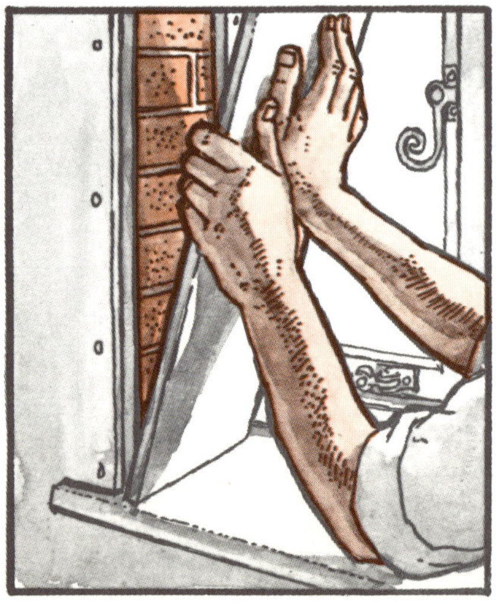

For dry lining, screw a framework of battens to the wall. The battens will have to coincide with the edges of the wallboard when it is fixed. Check for horizontal and vertical alignment with a straight-edge. Where necessary, use packing pieces to bring the battens true.

Around windows, fireplaces and recesses arrange a framework of battens. In these areas smaller pieces of cut board will be used.

Dry lining In older houses, especially, it is not unusual for the plaster to be in such a poor state, that the whole lot has to be scraped off back to bare bricks.

Here a new plaster surface can be created using Gyproc wallboard fixed to battens. This is called dry lining, i.e. little or no water is used. Wallboard can be cut with an ordinary handsaw.

The boards have a paper surface, so be careful not to tear this when nailing the boards to the battens. Your supplier will advise on the correct nails to use.

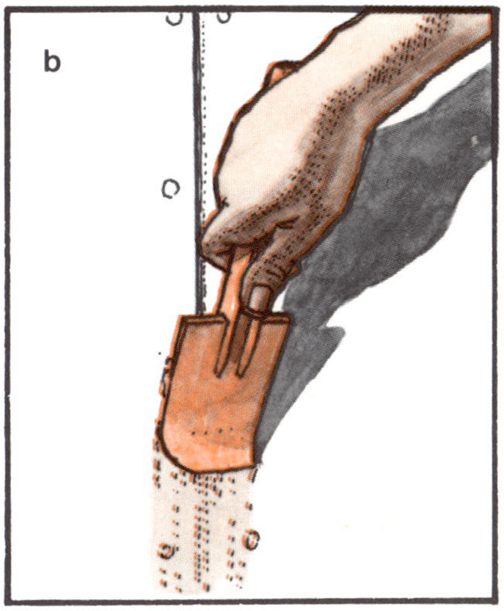

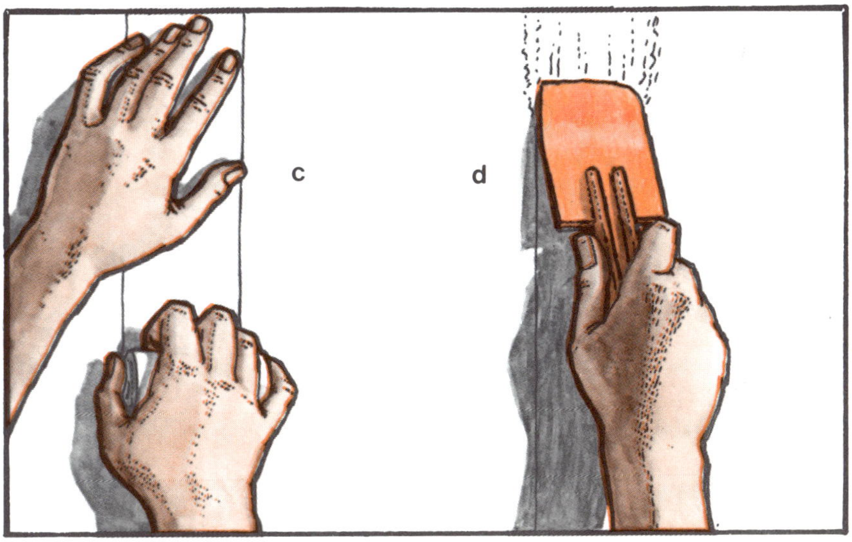

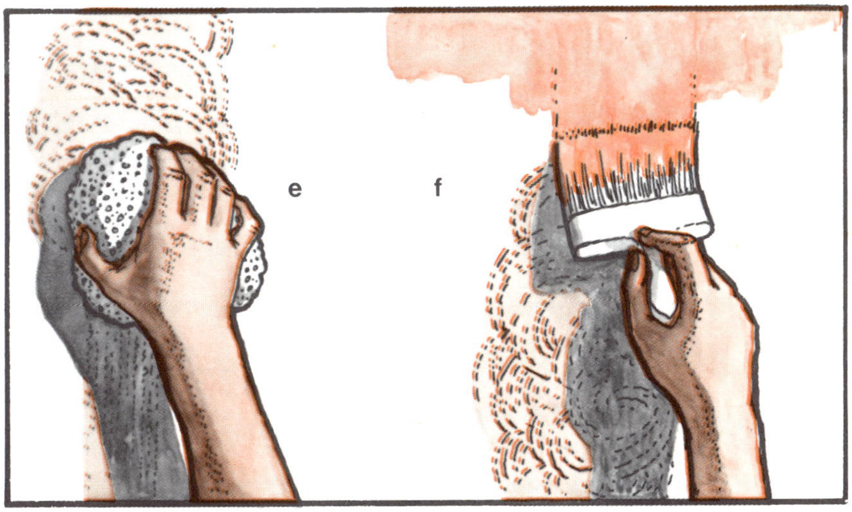

Cut each board about 1$\frac{1}{2}$in. less than room height. Lift them into position with a simple foot-lifter made from softwood. Nail each board onto the backing battens at 6in. intervals. (a)

A special applicator is needed to fill the joints between the boards. Joint filler is used here – mixed according to the instructions on the packet. (b)

Press a complete length of joint tape down the joint, using a taping knife. (c)

Apply another band of filler over the tape immediately. Wipe off the surplus filler from the joint edges before it starts to set. (d)

Two bands of joint finish (mixed according to instructions supplied) should be applied with the applicator. The first layer should be about 8in. wide. Feather out the edges with a sponge, working in light, circular strokes. When this band is partially dry, apply a second band about 1in. wide all down. Repeat the above process. (e)

A final, thin coat of finish applied over the complete surface of the wallboards will even up the texture between the main surface and the joints. (f)

Dealing With Condensation

Damp and condensation are two of the greatest nuisances of winter. Wet patches appear on ceilings and walls, ruining decorations, while moisture runs down windows to form puddles on sills, eventually breaking up the paintwork and causing the wood to rot.

Damp and condensation are entirely different things though their effect is basically the same. Before remedial action can be taken, you have to establish which of the two is causing the trouble.

Condensation is caused by warm, moist air contacting a cool surface. Moisture on kitchen and bathroom windows or beads of water on ceramic wall tiles are the more obvious signs. Damp patches on living room walls is another tell-tale sign.

The air is moistened by such things as steam from cooking, washing, burning paraffin heaters – even breathing. These combine to raise the room temperature and load the air with water vapour. When this moist air contacts a cool surface, the water vapour condenses on it.

So on a cold day, streaming windows and damp patches on walls indicate condensation.

To combat condensation, four things can be done. Keep rooms warm, dispose of steam and water vapour, provide ventilation, and avoid cold surfaces.

The kitchen and bathroom should be the main places to watch as most of the troubles spring from there. An extractor fan fitted in a window will help to remove water-laden air.

The manufacturers of the fan will tell you the recommended thickness of glass needed to support a fan.

When cutting a circular hole for the fan with a glasscutter use a pre-made template as a guide. Make two concentric circles – the largest being the required size for the fan.

Score a series of criss-cross lines inside the smaller circle before tapping out the small squares formed, starting from the centre. Repeat the process on the larger circle until this glass is all tapped out.

If you have to fit new glass, ask your supplier to cut the hole for you.

Most fans are easily fitted in two or three stages. Follow individual makers' instructions closely.

Very cold bathroom walls can be kept warm by fitting a black tubular heater that operates at 60 watts per foot.

CEILINGS

Line the ceilings with expanded polystyrene tiles. These give good insulation value and resist condensa-

Fix flame retardant polystyrene ceiling tiles to bathroom and kitchen ceilings to reduce condensation forming.

Cut the tiles with a Stanley-type knife, held against a straight-edge. Press down firmly on the knife to make a clean cut. Spread the special adhesive all over the back of each tile before fixing in place.

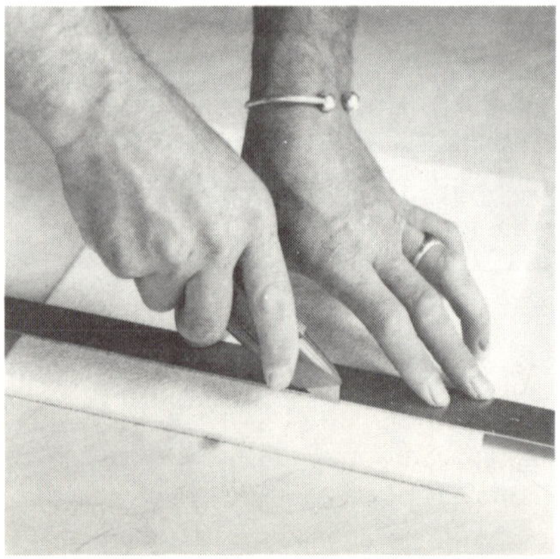

tion forming. Use flame-retardant types in kitchens or in any room where fire is a risk.

FIREPLACES

It is fashionable to block off fireplaces nowadays. The fireplaces used to provide ventilation; by blocking them in, ventilation is reduced or cut-off completely. Always allow for an air-brick when bricking up a fireplace. No flow of air in the chimney can cause damp patches on living room walls, especially on chimney breasts.

Paraffin or oil heaters contribute towards condensation problems. Radiators, electric convectors or radiant fires – any dry-heat types in fact – should be used. Even with these, however, correct ventilation is needed. An open window or a ventilator that can be controlled will enable you to allow the correct amount of air into the room according to the seriousness of the condensation problem.

WALLS

The simplest way to insulate walls against condensation is to line them with sheet expanded polystyrene which is sold in rolls at decorating shops. Wallpaper can be applied over the polystyrene in the normal way.

Cavity wall insulation is another method of wall insulation. This is discussed on page 24.

FLOORS

Less of a problem, usually, is condensation on solid floors. Many people imagine that damp patches are a sign of rising damp. There is a simple way to find out if they are.

Fix a small piece of glass to the floor with putty all round its edges so that air is trapped in the space between the glass and the floor.

If moisture forms on the bottom of the glass (after a short while) the problem is rising damp. If the moisture appears on the top of the glass, then you are up against condensation.

A good underlay beneath a carpet will help, as will a built-in foam underlay on any sheet material. Under linoleum or vinyl, fit a cork underlay or a reflective-faced building paper.

WINDOWS

Double glazing will help against, though may not always cure, condensation. The various systems are discussed more fully on page 24. Anyone with double glazing already installed who still gets condensation will find that some silica gel crystals (available from chemists) placed between the panes of glass will help. These absorb all the moisture, but they eventually become saturated and have to be dried out in an oven before re-use.

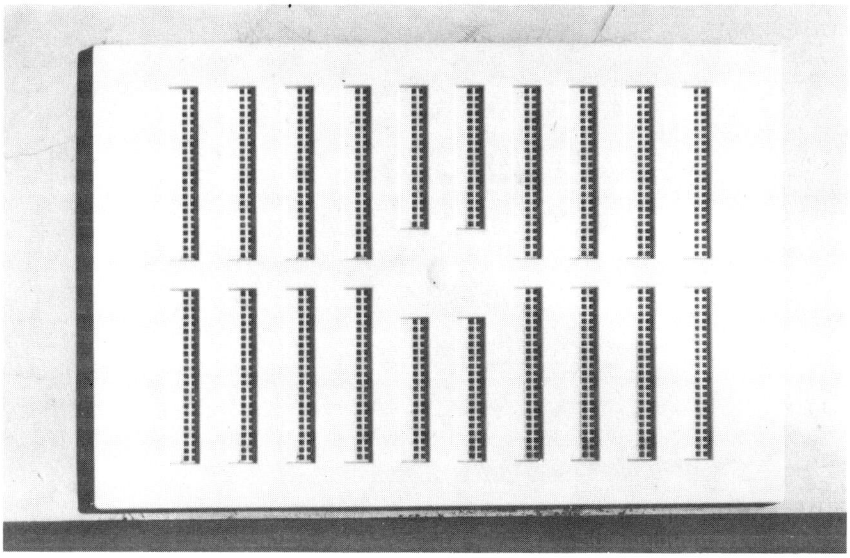

A blocked off chimney means it is no longer ventilated. Eventually damp patches will appear on the breast. An air brick or grill must be fitted in every room.
Mould, mildew or fungus on walls means having to strip off the wallpaper. Wash the wall with a fungicide before repapering, and use a paste containing a fungicide.

Walls affected by condensation should be lined with sheet expanded polystyrene. This is bought in rolls and can be papered over in the normal way.

Strip off the old wallcovering and hang the first length of polystyrene. Your supplier will advise you on the special adhesive needed to stick it to the wall. Use a roller to smooth out the length.

Trim with a sharp Stanley-type knife at the skirting and ceiling line.
Press down hard with the knife to cut the material cleanly. Carefully butt the edges of successive lengths.

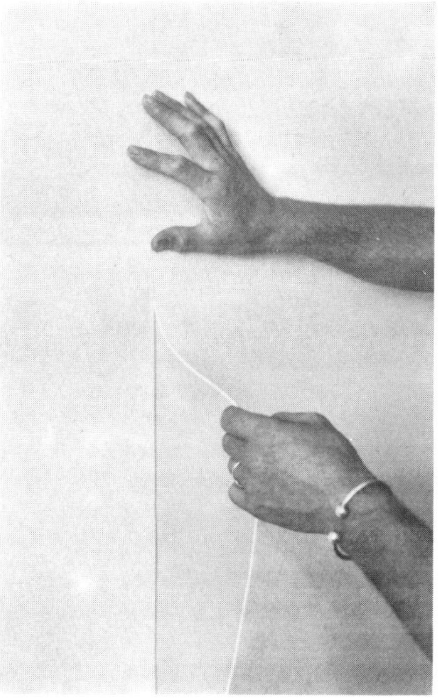

Dealing With Damp

If the weather is wet and muggy and damp patches appear on walls and floors then the problem is damp.

Damp is caused by such things as broken tiles (see page 46), defective flashings (see page 48), cracked down-pipes and gutters (see page 50). All these must be fixed immediately or the trouble will spread – it is no use redecorating hoping all will be well – it won't.

Usually the rain which is absorbed by the house walls dries out when the weather is dry. Sometimes, however, the water reaches the interior house walls. This can happen for a number of reasons.

Most modern houses are built with cavity walls, that is an inner and outer wall separated by an air cavity. The two walls are held together with steel ties. Normally there is no way that rainwater can cross the cavity and reach the inside wall (the steel ties are constructed to prevent them forming a 'bridge'). However, if, during wall construction, mortar is allowed to drop on to the ties a 'bridge' will be formed and the rainwater will cross.

Painting the outside wall with a silicone water repellent is the answer here. This seals the brickwork against rain but still allows the bricks to breathe so that trapped moisture vapour can escape.

Not all solid walls give rise to damp problems but many do. The more exposed walls facing the prevailing winds from the south-west are most likely to be affected. Damp patches in severe cases could extend over an entire internal wall.

Here again, a coat of silicone water repellent will help.

Other safeguards against water penetration are to make sure the pointing between the bricks is in good condition (see page 4), and any exterior grade decorative paint will also help.

Gaps around windows must be sealed. These gaps round a wooden window frame will widen and narrow as the frame expands and contracts

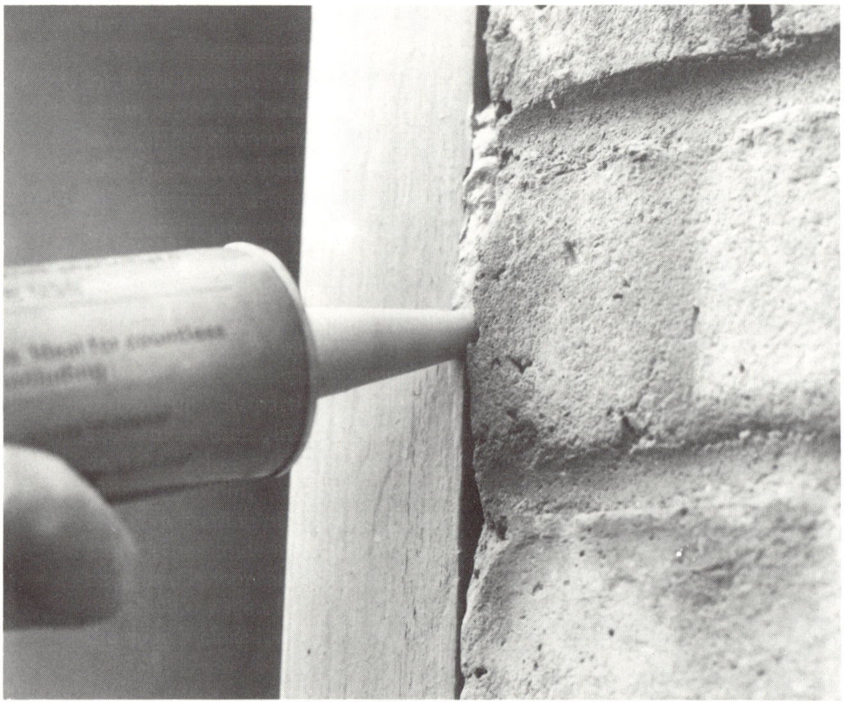

If the brickwork of the house walls is porous and the wall ties in the cavity between the inner and outer walls were covered with mortar droppings when the walls were built, then the ties form 'bridges' for rainwater to cross to the inside wall. Brush a proprietary damp-resisting liquid, usually silicone solution, on to the outside wall.

Seal any gaps between door and window frames and brickwork with a proprietary flexible mastic sealer. Do not use cellulose filler as this will crack and eventually fall out due to normal movement of the timber frame.

in its normal seasonal movement. It is no use filling them with Polyfilla or other cellulose filler; this will crack up and fall out after a short while. Use a mastic compound. This material is flexible and will expand and contract along with the frame, thus keeping the gaps permanently sealed.

DAMP-PROOF COURSES

The damp-proof course in the house wall prevents damp rising above the first few brick courses. Take a look at the lower part of the wall; you should see a horizontal layer of material set into the pointing.

This material spans both walls of the cavity and is usually slate or bitumen felt. It continues, unbroken, around all the walls. Normally damp will be stopped when it reaches the damp-proof course. However, should earth be piled up against the wall or a path raised too near the damp-proof course level there could be problems. The damp-proof course will be bridged and moisture from the earth will soak into the bricks. In heavy rain, water could splash up above it from the raised path.

So keep earth piles away from the house wall and make sure that the damp-proof course is at least 6in. above the level of paths. If you have to, then lower the level of a path by break-it up and re-laying it. Or else apply cement to the house wall to form a skirting. The cement must contain a waterproof agent, but whatever you do, it is worth while applying a water repellent liquid to the wall as well.

If the existing damp-proof course is faulty there are several firms who will carry out one of a number of methods of curing the trouble. Their addresses are in the yellow pages directory.

You can do the job yourself, though, using a damp repelling liquid – Stroma is one make. There are two grades – one for the inside walls and one for the outside walls. This liquid forms a barrier by penetrating right through the brickwork.

In older properties there may not be a damp-proof course at all. In days past, builders often relied on the thickness of materials to prevent rising damp – and often it did not work. The firms referred to above will help here, but they use systems which have to be carried out by specialists.

Rising damp can be caused by earth piled against the house wall over the level of the damp proof course or by a blocked airbrick. If these are not the causes get specialist advice.

Insulation

The heat generated in a house is lost through several places – roofs, walls, windows, floors, chimneys, doors and odd gaps around door and window frames. Since fuel bills are forever rising it makes sense to consider insulating the house properly. Most insulation methods must be regarded as a long-term investment. If the work is done properly, then fuel bills will be reduced.

The length of time it takes to recoup the initial outlay will depend on various factors – the size of the house and its position, whether all the 'escape routes' have been sealed effectively, and so on.

Double glazing, one aspect of insulation, is discussed on page 24. Here we are looking at the cheapest and simplest methods of insulation for roofs and ceilings, and around windows and doors.

Because warm air rises, a good deal of the heat in a house is lost through the roof. Without insulated ceilings, the heat will rise into the loft and, if the roof is not lined, it will go out through the tiles.

INSULATING A LOFT

Whether or not you insulate ceilings to keep the warm air in bedrooms depends on whether the loft is being used as a living space. If it remains empty, except for storage, you should insulate and there are three good alternatives. Laying loose-fill materials between the joists in the loft is an easy job. Loose-fill materials are such things as vermiculite, expanded polystyrene (granulated) and glass fibre and mineral wool. The insultant value of each type is about the same. If there is an advantage in using one or the other then it is probably dependent on the shape and layout of the loft space. If there are lots of nooks and crannies, the pellets or granules will probably be easier to pour into place. These are also best used when the spacings between the joists are not standard.

However in a windy loft space they can get blown about whereas a blanket will stay put.

Use foam plastic lagging to cover all pipework. Ask your builder's merchant for the right diameter to suit the size of your pipes. The foam has a split along its length so that it can be fitted quickly on to the pipe, and be taped in position.

All joins between pieces of lagging can be sealed with a waterproof plastic adhesive tape. Use the tape to seal any gaps in the foam which open at bends in the pipework.
Cut a T-shape plywood spreader to even out pellets or granules. These should be laid between the joists to an even depth of at least 3in.
Use a broom or the back of a rake to get into awkward corners.

A 3in. layer of vermiculite or expanded polystyrene is preferable. The material, supplied in bags, is poured between the joists and levelled out to the required thickness.

The alternatives are glass fibre and mineral wood in blanket form, which are laid between the joists.

The fibre blanket is sold in rolls about 45in. long and 16 to 18in. wide. Being comprised of glass or other mineral fibres, it can be irritating to the skin so gloves should be worn if you are so affected.

If the situation demands it, there is nothing to prevent using the blanket in one area and the pellets in another more inaccessible spot.

There is another form of blanket – quilt material which is draped over the joists. Here though, since the joists will be obscured, boards will have to be nailed over some of them to walk on when using the loft.

Whichever method you use, do not insulate the area immediately under the cold water tank. The warm air current must be allowed through from below to prevent this freezing. Finally, fix some insulation on the loft side of the trap door. These trap doors are of considerable area and account for much heat loss.

In addition to insulating the loft, you can stick expanded foam polystyrene tiles on the ceilings of rooms immediately below. However, while these are quite acceptable in kitchens and bathrooms, not everyone likes to see them in bedrooms. An alternative is to use more expensive tiles such as cork or fibre.

When heat is prevented from getting into the loft, it is important to insulate all the loft plumbing with lagging material. The loft will be much colder than before and, in winter, frozen pipework becomes more of a possibility.

If the loft space is to be used for living purposes, it will need to receive heat from the rooms below. So there is no point in insulating the ceiling or loft floor. So, the main concern is the roof itself. Modern roofs are usually underfelted. In older houses an alternative is to pin building paper to the rafters.

Where the loft is to be decorated, plasterboard or insulating board should be fixed to the rafters over the building paper.

Remember, though, there must always be sufficient space between the insulation material and the roof to ensure that rot does not form on the rafters.

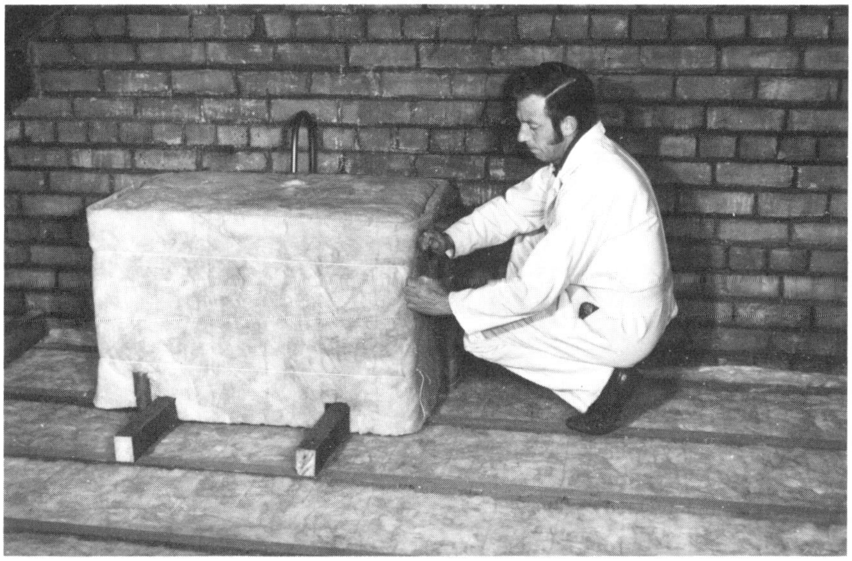

Starting at the eaves, tuck the blanket well down so that wind cannot blow underneath.
Unroll the length, tucking the edges up against the sides of the joists.
When the end of the loft is reached, tear off the blanket and again tuck the end down into the eaves.

Cover the ceiling hatch with a square of blanket. Glue it in place with pva adhesive. Do not cover the floor under the cold water tank – the heat that comes up from the room below will help prevent it freezing in cold weather. The tank itself can be lagged with strips of blanket.

PLUMBING –
FROST PROTECTION

All pipework and the cold water tank should be insulated to prevent freeze-ups in cold spells. A hot water cylinder must also be insulated to prevent heat escaping and thereby increasing fuel bills.

Wrap a blanket of glass fibre around the cold water tank and a specially made insulating jacket around the hot water cylinder. These jackets are available from most plumbers' merchants and are simply tied in place.

DRAUGHTS

Gaps around window and door frames can cause considerable discomfort from draughts apart from allowing valuable heat to escape, and it is amazing how much cold air can come through letterboxes and even keyholes. The solution here is to fix special flaps (available from d-i-y shops) to both the insides of letterboxes and keyholes.

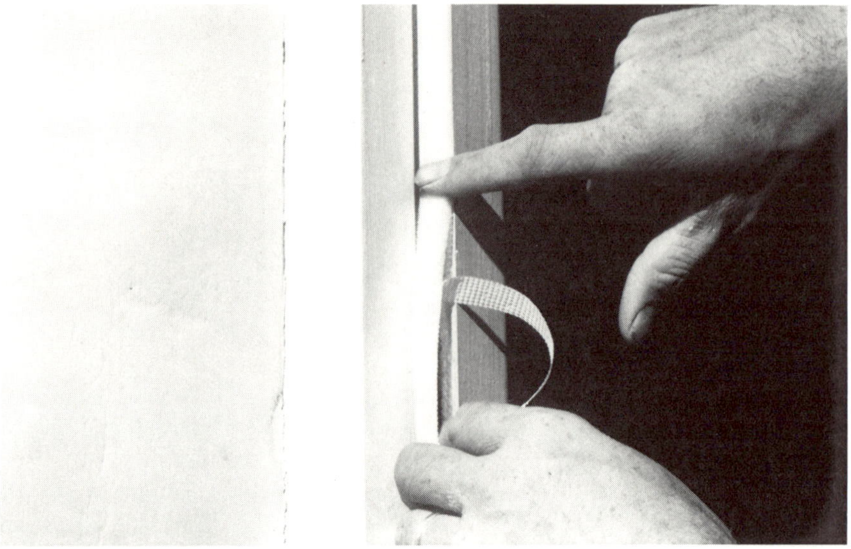

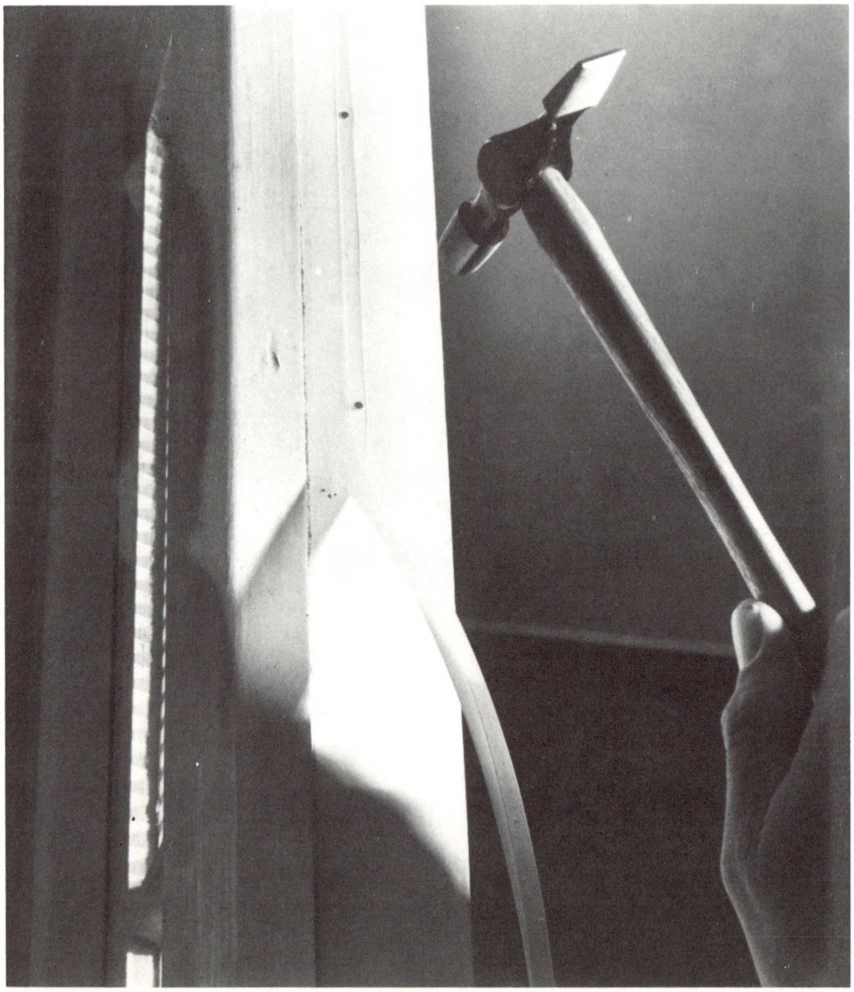

Plastic strips are the cheapest. They usually have to be replaced each year though. Just peel off the backing paper, cut to length with scissors, and stick them to the frame. This type will only effectively block normal gaps. Wide gaps can be blocked off using two plastic strips which come together when the door or window is closed.

Plastic strips with a layer of felt at the bottom are stuck in place after removing the protective paper backing. Cut to length with scissors.
Spring metal strip or a different kind of plastic strip can be tacked around the door or window rebate. It is not seen when the door is closed. Cut to length with scissors or wire cutters.

There are several draughtproofing systems available for sealing gaps around door and window frames.

The cheapest system (and the simplest to fix) is self-adhesive rubber or foam strips. When bought, these have a protective covering on the back which is peeled off and the strip is then stuck to the frame after making sure it is clean and dry. These strips are not suitable for sash windows.

Aluminium or phosphor bronze strips are also effective. These are fixed to the frames and then bent outwards. The door or window closes against the strip thus forming a tight seal.

They are slightly more difficult to fit since accuracy of positioning is essential and care must be taken to ensure that no kinks are formed in the metal.

Special draught excluders are made for metal windows though foam plastic strips will be adequate provided the metal is clean before sticking them on. Gaps under doors are notorious for letting through draughts. Though a $\frac{1}{4}$in. thick batten nailed across the threshold often forms an efficient seal (provided that carpets of the same thickness are used on both sides of the door to prevent people tripping over the batten), it can look unsightly and will only be partly effective if the gap is more than $\frac{1}{4}$in. Commercial draught excluders are made from rubber mouldings, aluminium section or a combination of metal and plastic. Other types come in halves – one being fixed to the door, and other to the threshold – which lock together when the door is closed.

Seal metal windows with a proprietary aluminium strip system available at d-i-y shops. The strip clips to the outside of the frame and is secured with corner pieces.

A threshold strip can be fixed to the floor.

Rise and fall draught excluders are available where the door has to clear a door mat. These are very effective though they can be tricky to position correctly.

UNDERFLOOR DRAUGHTS

Although a flow or air under timber floors is essential to prevent rot, the draughts that can come up through the floorboards can cause a lot of discomfort.

Filling gaps in floorboards is discussed on page 38. Here, it is worth saying that mastic can be used to plug any minor gaps.

WALL INSULATION

The walls of a house are the biggest cause of heat loss. All building materials have a U value. This, in essence, represents the measure of heat loss – the higher the U value, the lower the insulation value of a material.

For example, a sealed-cavity 11in. external wall, plastered on one side, has a U value of ·30. If $\frac{1}{2}$in. insulating fibreboard fixed to battens replaces the plaster, the U value would be ·18. However, if the cavity were filled with insulating material such as mineral wool or foam, the U value would be ·09 and ·07 respectively.

So you can see from this how beneficial the cavity wall insulation materials are. Assuming that all other insulating work is carried out as well, the claim that cavity wall insulation could reduce fuel bills substantially does not seem unreasonable.

There are two systems of cavity wall insulation which will reduce heat losses through walls by about 70%.

Rentokil Limited uses dry mineral rock wool blown into the cavity and packed to a uniform density. The other system, used by many manufacturers, involves urea formaldehyde foam, which is pumped into the cavity where it sets in the form of an insulating layer.

Side benefits of this type of insulation are that the house walls will be free from damp and condensation. Damp will not rise through capillary action since both materials are water repellent.

Cavity wall insulation is not a d-i-y job, however. It should be carried out by professionals, using an approved material. The actual work usually takes a day to complete in an average size house. Holes are drilled in the mortar joints between the bricks to allow the material to be injected. At the end of the day, the contractors will fill in the holes leaving the walls looking as they did before.

Solid walls Of course cavity infill can only be used if there is a cavity between the house walls. External 9in.-thick solid brick walls need to be lined for proper insulation.

One method is to fix $\frac{1}{2}$in.-thick insulation boards to the plaster, and then plaster over the boards. Alternatively, the insulation boards can be hidden behind plasterboard, hardboard or plywood. The boards can be of non-combustible fibre or polystyrene. Decorative insulating boards are available which would not need to be covered with anything else. Plain boards, though, have the advantage that they can be painted or papered and your choice of colour or design is not limited.

A second method of dealing with solid walls is to nail insulating quilt material to battens fixed to the walls. Fix more battens over the quilt and fix insulating fibre board to the battens.

DOUBLE GLAZING

Because of rising fuel bills, more and more people are installing double glazing to reduce heat losses and increase comfort in the home.

It should be said that double glazing alone will not reduce fuel bills dramatically. It has to be used in conjunction with other insulating methods discussed on page 16.

Assuming you attend to the other forms of insulation, which are comparatively cheap, the types of double glazing available and their benefits can be considered.

The heat generated in a house escapes through various channels. In an average size semi, insulated to current minimum standards of Building Regulations, with a window area of about 20% of the total area of the external walls, the windows account for 22% of heat losses.

Double glazing cuts the heat loss through the windows by 50%, that is, the heat loss from the house through the windows is cut to 11%. Thus 11% of the cost of the heat generated in the house can be saved, meaning a minimum saving of £11 per £100 heating costs. Of course, this is not a hard and fast rule since so many variations in house design are to be found.

Actual fuel cost savings, therefore, depend on several factors. For example, if a house has more than 20% area of outside glazing, then proportionately more heat escapes through the windows.

Therefore by halving these larger heat losses, double glazing will be reducing the fuel bill proportionately more. Similarly, if the house is surrounded by open spaces, or is in an enclosed urban area, this can affect heat losses and therefore, in turn, affect the heat cost reductions which can be achieved.

The human element must also be considered. Control of a central heating system does affect the amount of heat that needs to be generated to maintain an even, warm temperature.

Cold windows Double glazing can also provide other benefits to make a house more comfortable. It reduces cold down draughts from the window; eliminates the cold window area of a room thus enlarging living space; reduces noise irritation and controls condensation.

So there should be no more huddling around the fire, or radiators, and using only a small part of the room that is not cold.

Noise The reduction of noise level entering the room from outside is a really valuable asset of double glazing. Excessive noise can cause stress, in extreme cases mental disorder and temporary loss of vision, and lack of proper sleep.

For sound-insulation the main factors to be considered are:
(a) the elimination of gaps and cracks both in the complete window assembly and in the fixing into the main structure;
(b) the space between the two panes of glass;
(c) the weight of the glass – in general, the thicker the better.

When secondary sash (double window) systems are installed to achieve sound insulation, the efficiency of the system is increased if the sides of the air space are lined with sound absorbent materials.

The minimum air space between the two panes in double glazing should be 4in., although an air space of 8in. is generally the optimum for sound insulation.

Now let us look at the types of double glazing that are available. Double glazing can be either a complete, hermetically sealed replacement unit or an additional secondary window. The main systems are:

Insulating glass: A factory-made, hermetically sealed double glazing unit which requires cleaning on two sides only (as with ordinary glazed windows). There are two kinds:

The standard type looks like a single sheet of glass but in fact consists of two pieces of glass joined together with a sealed metal, alloy or plastic edge, and is usually purpose-made. The air between the two panes is dried to prevent misting. In existing houses, it may be necessary to alter the rebates of the window frames for a neat appearance. Installing this type is not really a job for an amateur.

The second type (a stepped-unit) is a modified version of the previous unit, with one glass bigger all round than the other. It is ideal for converting single glazed frames to double glazing without altering the frame. Good draught-proofing of opening window frames adds to the effectiveness of both types of insulating glass.

Secondary sashes This is a simple system whereby a second pane of glass is added within the existing window openings and is tailor-made. It can be fixed, sliding or hinged. A glazed secondary sash is usually removable and can be lifted out of the surrounding framework for cleaning. This type can usually be installed without disturbing the original window.

A third system is called *coupled windows*: Here a single glazed window has another window coupled to it so that both move together. Fitted with hinges and fasteners, the frames can be separated for cleaning. A coupled window is more often specified for new buildings although they can be used to improve existing homes provided modifications are made to the original surrounds. Secondary sashes and coupled windows are generally more suitable for sound-insulation.

Last of all is a simple and cheap *do-it-yourself* system which uses flexible channels to hold the second pane of glass, the glass itself being obtained separately from glass merchants.

The makers supply various types of channels which can easily be cut to the required size. Special clips and screws are provided and, after the glass has been fixed inside the channel, it is a simple matter to fix the secondary sash to the original frame or surround.

Manufacturers of double glazing systems like this will provide assembly and fixing instructions.

When deciding on the type to use, consider the window's location in relation to prevailing winds, safety and the design and strength of the primary window.

For up-to-date costs of double glazing get estimates from individual manufacturers. The Insulation Glazing Association will advise you further if you need help in choosing the correct system. They will also provide a list of member firms whom you can contact for estimates.

The secondary sash is easily fixed with special clips.

Taps and Stop-cocks

Taps An annoying trickle of water from the cold tap over the kitchen sink when it is turned tightly off indicates that a new washer is needed.

Re-washering a tap is avoided by many people because they envisage a sudden uncontrollable flood of water pouring from the dismantled tap. Yet it is an easy enough operation.

The first thing you must do – to prevent that 'uncontrollable flood' – is to turn off the main stop-cock which usually is found under the sink, though it could be in a purpose-made pit outside the house. No doubt, though, you will know where your stop-cock is situated. Turn it off completely. Now turn the kitchen sink tap on fully and wait until no more water gushes out.

Your kitchen tap may have an easy clean cover and usually this will unscrew by hand after unscrewing the top.

Next, use a padded wrench to grip the lower part of the tap's body; use another wrench to grip the nut securing the headgear and remove it.

Inside will be the jumper. The washer will be attached to it. Grip the stem of the jumper with a wrench and remove the nut that holds the washer in place.

Position the new washer and replace the nut to secure it. You can then re-assemble the tap and turn on the water again.

Sometimes the nut cannot be removed easily. The best solution here is to fit a new jumper and washer.

If a tap over the sink has a shrouded head, simply remove this and proceed as before. It will probably be necessary to use a screwdriver to prise off the plastic tab on the head of the tap (which has a small C, for cold on it) in order to reach the screw holding the shrouded head in place.

Bathroom taps usually have a slightly different arrangement. The jumper and washer is pegged into the headgear. This is necessary since the low pressure of water under which they operate may not be enough to raise the jumper when the tap is turned on.

Unscrew the nut holding the jumper and washer together. Remove them both and replace with a new jumper and washer.

Since the new jumper will not be pegged into the headgear, it might be necessary to taper the stem of the jumper so that it will fit tightly in the headgear.

Before re-washering bathroom taps (whether hot or cold the method is the same) there is no need to turn off the main stop valve. If there is a stop valve on either the cold supply pipe to the hot water cylinder or on the cold supply pipes to the bathroom taps, turn off which ever is appropriate depending on which tap you are re-washering.

If there are no stop valves, then tie up the ball valve to the main cold storage tank and then drain the tank.

There is no need to switch off the immersion heater or turn out the boiler provided, that is, that the hot water system has been properly designed.

A final word on bathroom taps, in fact on all mixer taps. For re-washering purposes these can be thought of as two independent taps to be re-washered as before. Just ascertain from the spout which tap is dripping after it has been turned off. This is simple to do since the spout is partitioned down its middle.

STOP-COCKS

If the stop-cock starts to leak it can be repaired easily. The leaking water is by-passing the gland packing. By turning the first nut through which the spindle of the tap passes (called the gland adjusting nut) the drip will be stopped. Half a turn or perhaps one full turn is usually enough.

After the gland nut has been adjusted over a period of time, the packing inside will have to be renewed. Screw down the stop-cock to prevent the water from flowing past and release the screw holding the handle in place.

Completely unscrew the gland nut and remove it. Rake out all the old packing and replace with knitting wool coated with Vaseline. Pack it down tightly before replacing the gland nut and handle.

The workings of a tap.

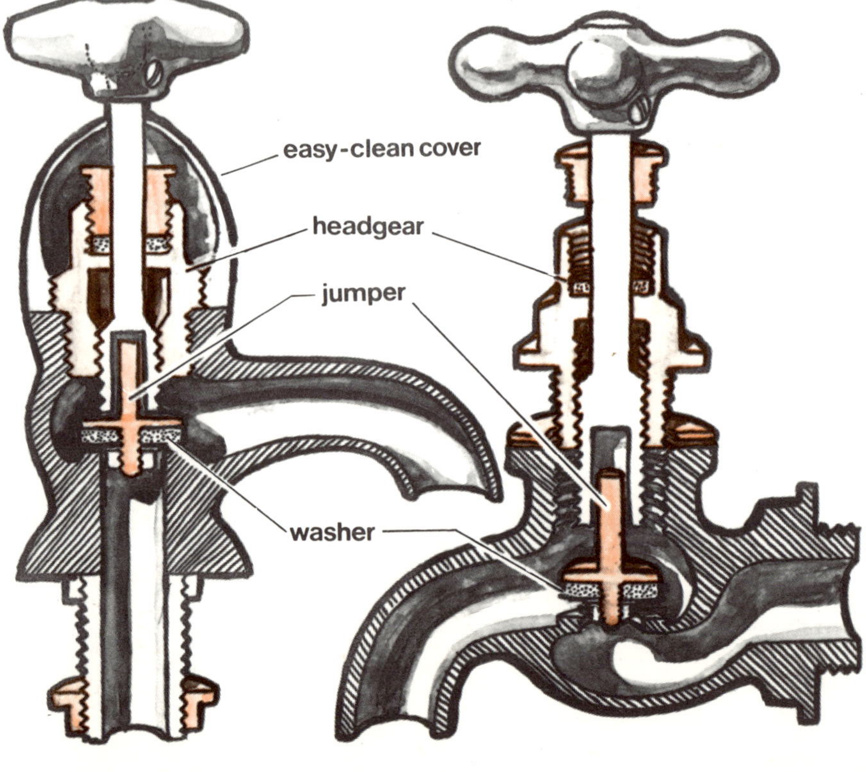

Keeping Drains in Order

The underground drains in a house drainage system are laid in straight lines at a slight gradient. Since they can become blocked from time to time, every part of the underground system must be accessible to drain rods so that they can be cleared.

Near the house there will be an inspection chamber (or manhole) to take the branch drains from the yard gulley and the house soil pipe. The branch drains connect to a 4in. diameter drain which runs to another chamber probably situated just inside the garden boundary.

If the house is an older one, the inspection chamber nearest the house could have an intercepting trap fitted, which is intended to prevent rats and sewer gases entering the house. It impedes drainage, however and is the likely cause of blockages.

If the water in the w.c., sinks or basins drain away slowly, or if a water gully overflows, check this first chamber initially. It is the most likely trouble spot.

Normally a blockage here can be cleared easily, using drain rods which can usually be hired locally. A plunger (a 4in. diameter rubber disc) is screwed to the end of the rods to do the work.

Above the entrance to the trap there will be a stopper fitted into the end of a rodding arm. This arm enables blockages between the intercepting trap and the sewer to be cleared.

Sometimes, the stopper can fall out of the arm into the trap causing a blockage. A simple way to avoid this re-occurring is to cement a small glass disc in place of the stopper. If ever access to the rodding arm is needed the disc can be broken and replaced with another.

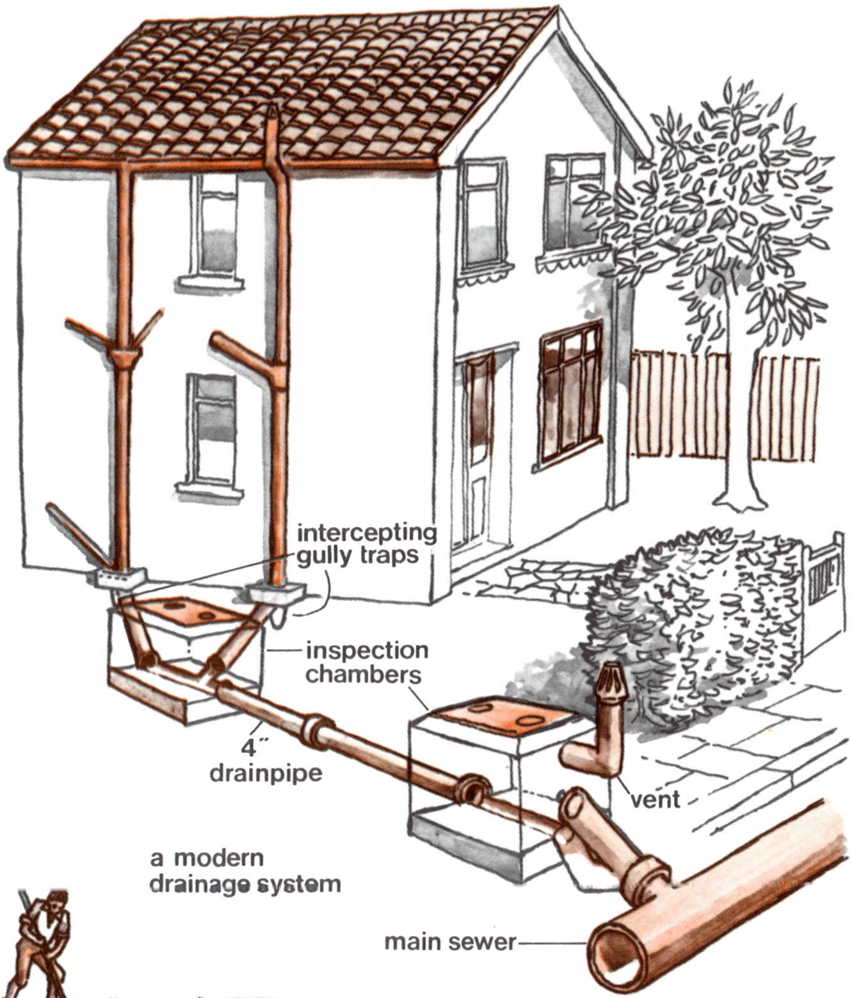

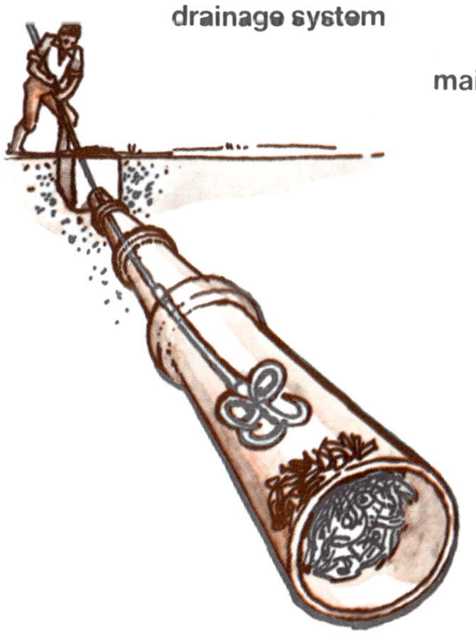

Screw two drain rods together. Fit a corkscrew head and push the rods down the manhole. Never turn the rods anti-clockwise or they will become unscrewed in the drain. If more than one drainpipe enters the manhole, push the rods down each one until the blockage is clear.

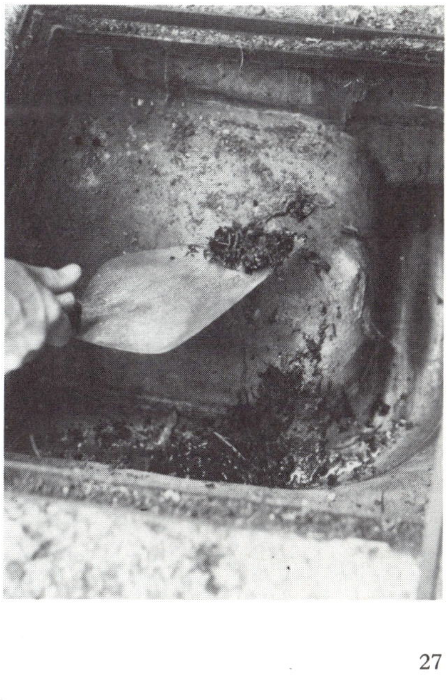

Remove with a trowel any rubbish which collects in the manhole.

Most blockages in the sink waste pipes are easily cleared with a plunger. It is worth while buying one of these and they are often inexpensive. Stuff the overflow outlet in the sink with a wet rag. Position the plunger over the drain hole and let about 1in. of water into the sink; then pump vigorously. The water will usually drain away quickly.

More stubborn blockages occur when the U bend of the waste pipe below the sink gets filled with matchsticks, hair, or other rubbish. Modern plastic pipe fittings are easy to deal with and normally only a U bend section or a bottle trap has to be unscrewed and cleaned out.

Old metal pipework can be more of a problem. In the bottom of the U bend is a drain plug which can be difficult to budge. An old chisel will often give sufficient leverage to move it.

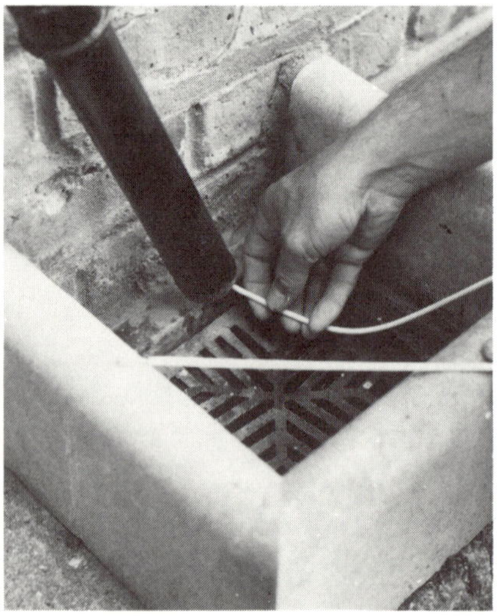

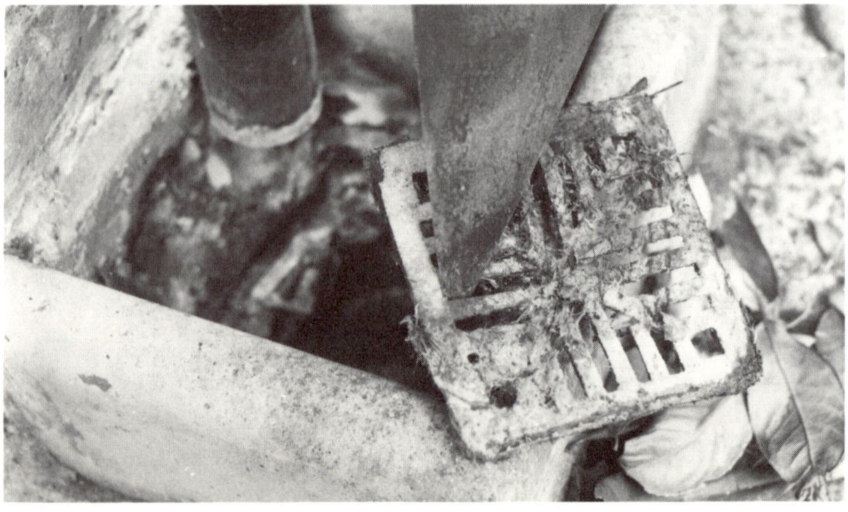

A plunger will clear most blockages. When removing a bottle trap, U bend or drain plug, keep a bucket underneath to catch the sink water as it gushes out.

A really stubborn plug in old pipework may need a wrench to budge it.

If, after removing the bottle trap, U bend or drain plug, the blockage still does not clear, feed a flexible curtain wire fitted with an eye down into the waste outlet of the sink and prod away the obstruction.

If a blockage is in the waste pipe on the other side of the U bend, feed the curtain wire into the waste pipe from outside the house.

The grid over the outside drain can become blocked by leaves and other debris. This can cause drains to smell. Lift out the grid and burn off all the debris by holding it over a fire made in the garden. Flush out the drain with hot water and soda before replacing the grid.

Doors New and Old

A door which jams in winter yet opens in summer is usually the result of humidity changes swelling and shrinking the timber. Minor problems could be caused by excessive coats of paint. In both cases the paint on the edge of the door will have to be stripped back to bare wood. With a plane, shave off a little more of this than necessary to ease the door to allow for the thickness of new paint.

Only paint when the timber is thoroughly dry. Remove the door from its hinges and apply two liberal coats of primer to both the top and bottom edges if it is these that are sticking. Allow to dry thoroughly and rehang.

High spots on the closing edge can always be located by closing the door over carbon paper. The areas showing marks along the edge can then be planed back after opening the door and holding it firm with wedges.

Loose hinges can cause a door to sag and not close properly. Try retightening the screws. If they remain loose, remove them, fill the holes with wood plugs and reinsert the screws. Check also that the hinges are set deep enough into the door and frame so that the gap is equal along

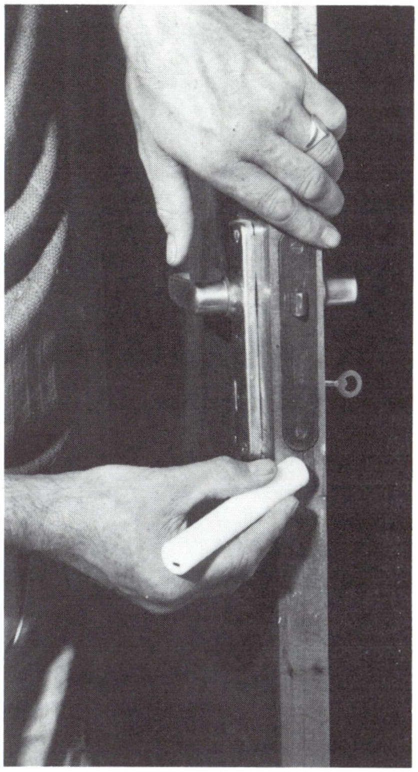

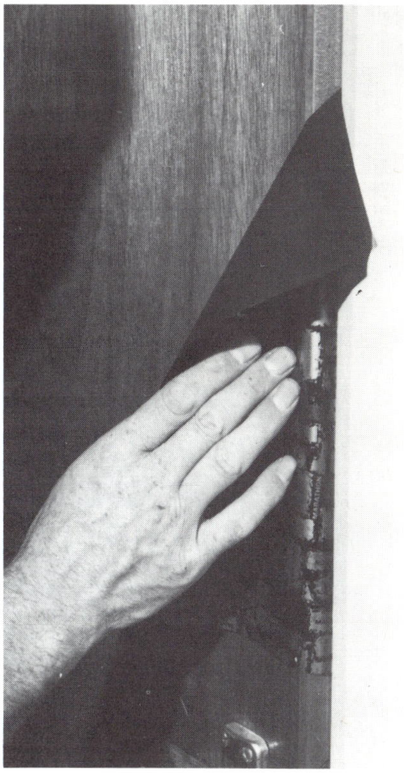

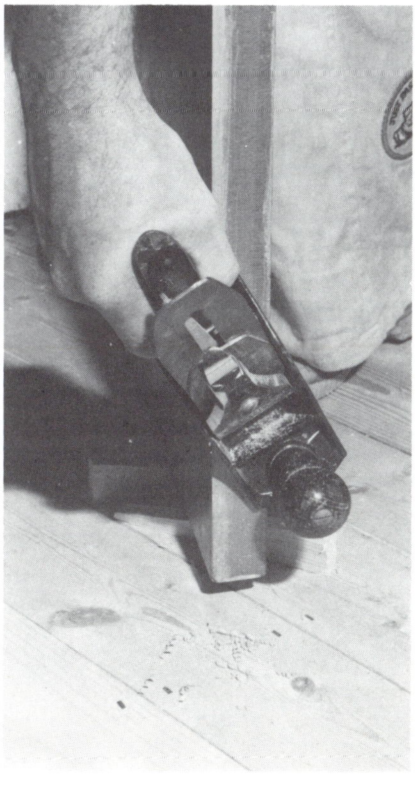

Minor sticking problems can often be cured by rubbing the closing edge with a candle.

Ascertain sticking points by closing the door on a sheet of carbon paper. The carbon will leave tell-tale marks.

Secure the door with wedges before planing back to bare wood.

Altering the position of hinges by cutting the hinge rebates deeper will cure too wide a gap on the hinged side of a close door. If the door is binding on the hinge side insert thin wood packing pieces into the hinge slots.

both vertical edges of the door when it is in the closed position. A wider gap down the hinge side may indicate that the hinge rebates require to be slightly deepened with a sharp chisel. If, however, the hinges have been set too deeply into both door and frame, they can be raised by removing the hinges and fitting one or more thicknesses of card under the hinge before screwing back into position.

Remember that large gaps can also be dealt with by fixing draught excluders to the frame surround.

RATTLING DOORS

Usually caused by the door catch not resting firmly against its stop. The latch keep (or strike plate) has to be repositioned nearer to the stop.

Carefully check the distance between door face and the door jamb on the lock side. Then remove the plate and extend the recess and mortice correspondingly with a sharp chisel, carefully keeping all edges of the cut timber square. Before screwing the plate back into position plug the original screw holes with timber.

Wide gaps can be overcome by fitting a weatherstrip or draught excluder (see page 22).

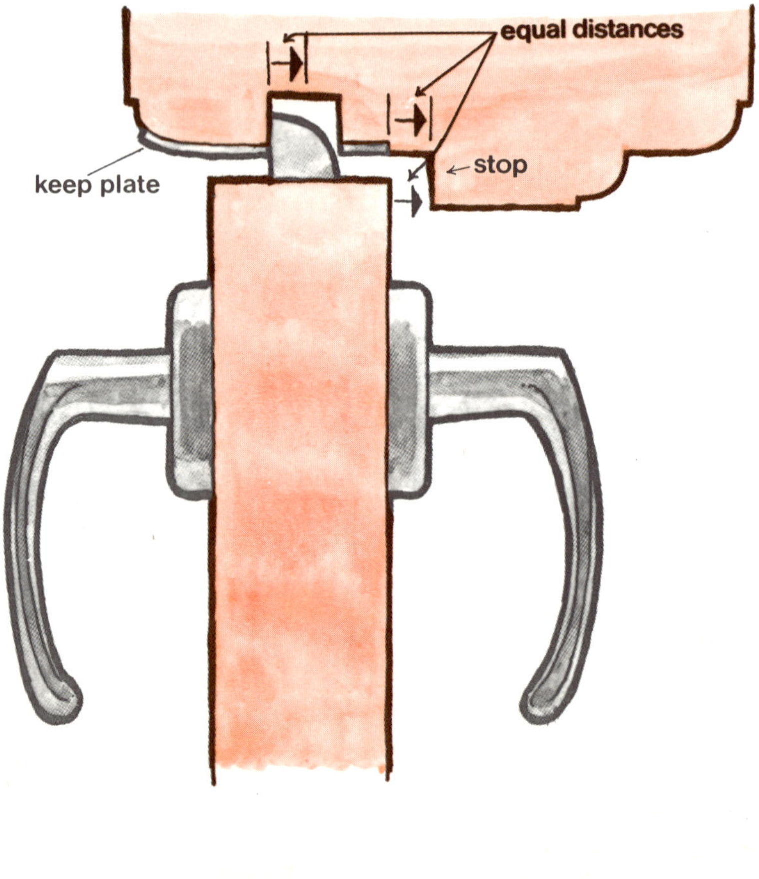

Measure the distance from the jamb to the face of the door. The keep plate must be moved back by this amount Remove the keep – it is screwed in place – and use a chisel to extend the existing recess to the required position. Extend the mortises as required. Refit the keep plate after first plugging the old screw holes with timber plugs.

PANELLING A DOOR

The simplest way to flush panel a door is to face it with hardboard or plywood, leaving a border around the perimeter. This obviates the need to cut new holes for the keyhole and handle in the facing material.

If hardboard or thin plywood is used to flush panel a door completely, the two long edges must be lipped with solid timber in order that the facing material does not rub or fray at the edges.

Completely flush panelling a door is made rather more complicated by having to reposition the door catch to allow for the extra thickness of the door and to accommodate the handle and lock. The door will have to be removed for this operation.

If you are using hardboard for the flush panel, this must be conditioned first to the room's atmosphere to prevent it buckling later on. This is done by damping the rough side of each sheet with water. Two pints to an 8ft. × 4ft. sheet is about right. Lay the sheets flat (wet side to wet side) for 24 hours in the room in which they are to be used.

Any loose or flaking paint must be removed from the face of the door and the surface rubbed down with fine glasspaper as a key for the adhesive.

As the door has already been removed fixing the panel will be easier if you lay it flat on the ground.

Apply a coat of primer to the facing material before painting.

Pack out all the panels with plywood to bring them level with the stiles and rails. Use pins and adhesive to fix the plywood and the facing panel to the door. Punch all pin heads below the surface. Fill all the pin holes with filler (such as Polyfilla). The door is now ready for priming and painting.

Flush panelling a door with hardboard or thin plywood will require lipping down both long edges. This will mean cutting new mortices and recesses for hinges and lock.

FITTING A NEW DOOR

If you have to fit a new door it must be exactly the same height, width and thickness as the old one. They are readily available from timber merchants and will be delivered with protective pieces (called horns) projecting from the top and bottom. Saw off these flush with the edges.

a

b

First remove the horns and then hold the door in the frame and mark off the outline of the frame on to the door, using a pencil. There should be an $\frac{1}{8}$in. gap between both sides of the door and the frame so remember to trim down slightly past the pencil lines. The top edge must also be trimmed to allow an $\frac{1}{8}$in. gap at the top and a sufficient gap at the bottom to clear the floorcovering by $\frac{1}{4}$in. (a)

Rest the door on battens to protect its edge and then plane down to just beyond the pencil lines. (b)

Hold the trimmed door in the frame and mark off the positions of the hinge slots.
When fitting a new door, use the old hinge recesses cut in the frame. Hold the new door in position in the frame and mark off the hinge positions on the door. Get help to keep the door raised while marking, or support it with wedges. (c)

c

d

Hold each hinge in position on the door and mark off its width and length. Scribe the lines about $\frac{1}{8}$in. deep, using a mortice gauge, or mark off accurately with a pencil. (d)

e

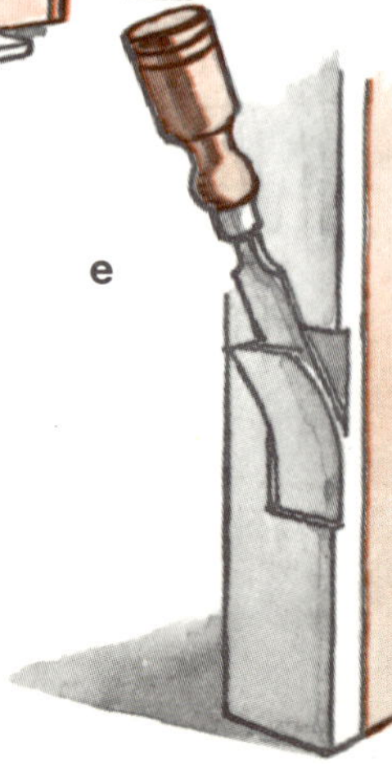

Use a chisel and hammer to chop out the hinge recesses. The hinge must lie flush with the surface. Use the chisel squarely against the timber when cutting – keeping the flat back of the chisel fractionally inside the line. A hammer can be used on the chisel if it has a plastic handle – otherwise use a mallet on a wooden handle chisel. (e)

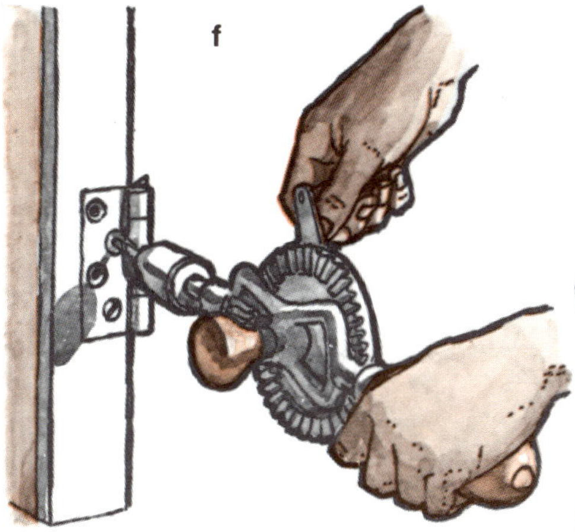

f

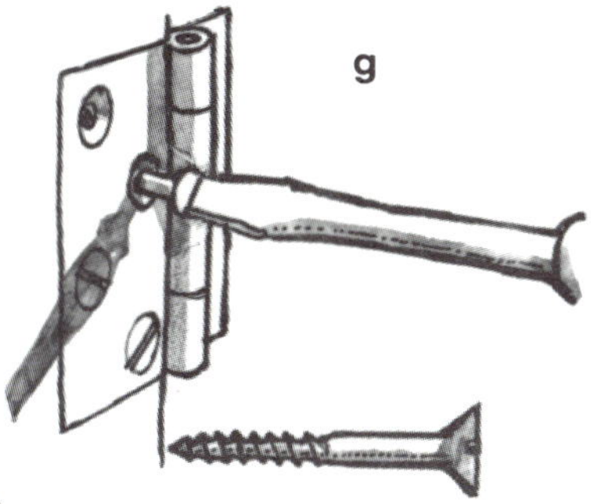

g

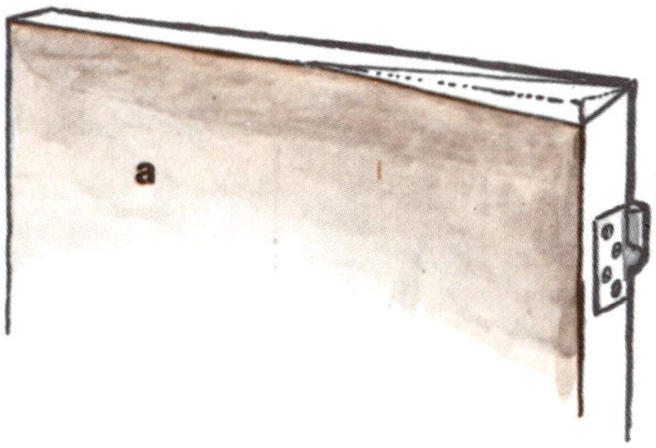

a

b

c

d

It is usually easier to fix the door furniture – lock, letterplate, etc., before hanging it. If it is to have glass panels, any glazing must be done after the door is in place.

You will probably have to trim a little off the door for it to fit the frame, as the frame may not be quite true.

Get a helper to hold the door in place while you mark off any trimming lines and the hinge positions. If help is not available to hold the door, a couple of wedges will provide support.

Remember to prime thoroughly and paint the bottom edge before hanging the door as, once in position, there will not be another opportunity to paint this edge again.

Drill starter holes for the screws to prevent them splitting the wood as they go in. (f)

Secure the hinges with 1½in. countersunk woodscrews. Countersunk screws are needed so that their heads do not protrude above the hinge surface to prevent it closing tightly. (g)

When fitting rising butts (see next page), mark off the top of the door where it meets the door stop. Mark off the centre of the door at the top; draw a diagonal line between this point and the door stop line on the hinge side. Plane off the waste material to leave a bevel to give the door clearance. (a)

Mark off the outline of the socket plate on the door. Scribe the lines with a cutting gauge, and chisel out the recess. (b)

Lift the door and lower the socket plate on to the spindle plate. (c)

Use only one screw initially in the frame side of each hinge in case adjustment of their positions is needed. Test that the door opens and closes freely before fixing remaining screws. (d)

HINGE MAINTENANCE

Since the hinges are the only things supporting a door, they must be of a sufficient size and be the correct type to take the weight of the door.

For exterior doors always use non-ferrous metal hinges to prevent rusting.

Hinges should be oiled regularly with only a little oil used on each occasion. Have a rag handy to wipe away any surplus oil that runs down the door. On outside hinges use grease rather than oil which will evaporate quickly.

LOCK MAINTENANCE

An easy way to lubricate cylinder locks (such as the Yale type) normally found on the front door is to drop a little oil on to the key before inserting it into the lock.

The spring of a conventional back-door lock needs greasing occasionally. You can get at the spring by taking the lock off the door and unscrewing the back plate. If it is a mortice lock, first remove the door handles and then withdraw the lock from the door. Then you can separate the lock casing.

RISING BUTTS

These are popular hinges because they automatically raise the door over a floorcovering as it opens.

They come in two parts; a spindle plate that fits to the door frame and a socket plate that fits on the door.

It will probably be necessary to fill the existing screw holes in both the frame and the door with small wood plugs as the positions of the new holes may not correspond.

FITTING A LETTER PLATE

A new letter plate is usually fixed to the middle rail or the stile of a new door.

The easiest way to cut an apperture in solid timber is to drill a hole in each corner of the proposed opening and then saw along each line in turn by inserting a padsaw into each of the holes.

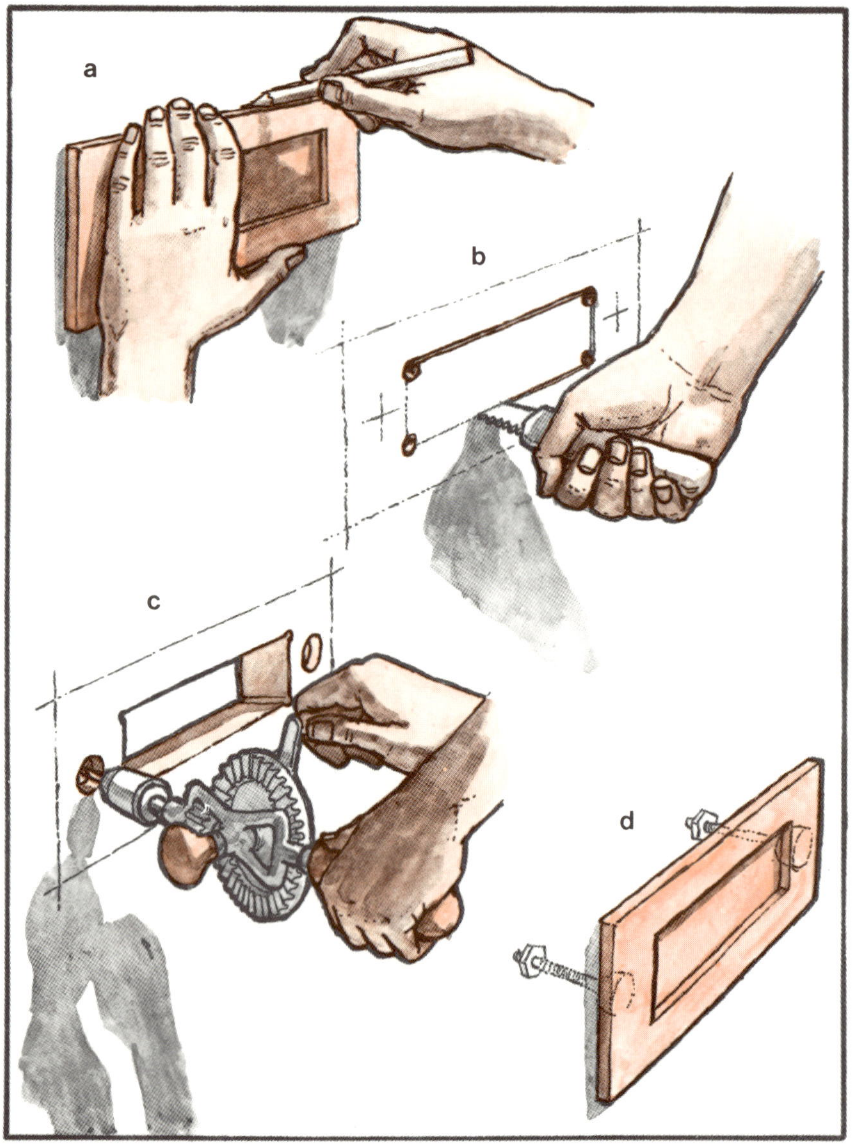

Pencil the outline of the letter plate on to the door (a). Drill holes through each corner of the slot through which the letters go. Cut along the pencil lines using a pad saw (b). Remember to position a block of wood on the reverse side of the door to prevent the drill bursting through and splitting the grain. It is easier to do this if the door is first removed and laid flat.

Hold the letter plate in position and mark off the positions of the sockets. Drill ½in. diameter holes, ½in. deep. In the centre of these, drill smaller holes right through the door the size of the letter plate bolts. (c)

Fit the letter plate and tighten the fixing nuts of the bolts. (d)

Ceiling Repairs and Ceiling Coving

MENDING A PLASTERBOARD CEILING

Mending a large hole in a plasterboard ceiling is not as difficult as it may sound.

Plasterboard is obtainable at builders' merchants. A new piece can be nailed to a softwood framework fixed to the joists above the ceiling.

Cut out the damaged area of plasterboard with a saw to form a square recess. The opposite sides of the opening should be cut flush with the internal face of the joists. (a)

A new softwood framework should be fixed to the joists. Nail the new plasterboard to the four sides of the framework, leaving a small gap at the edges. (b)

Spread a band of joint filler around the edges of the new plasterboard. (c) Then spread scrim tape along the edges. Proceed as for wall lining, page 15.

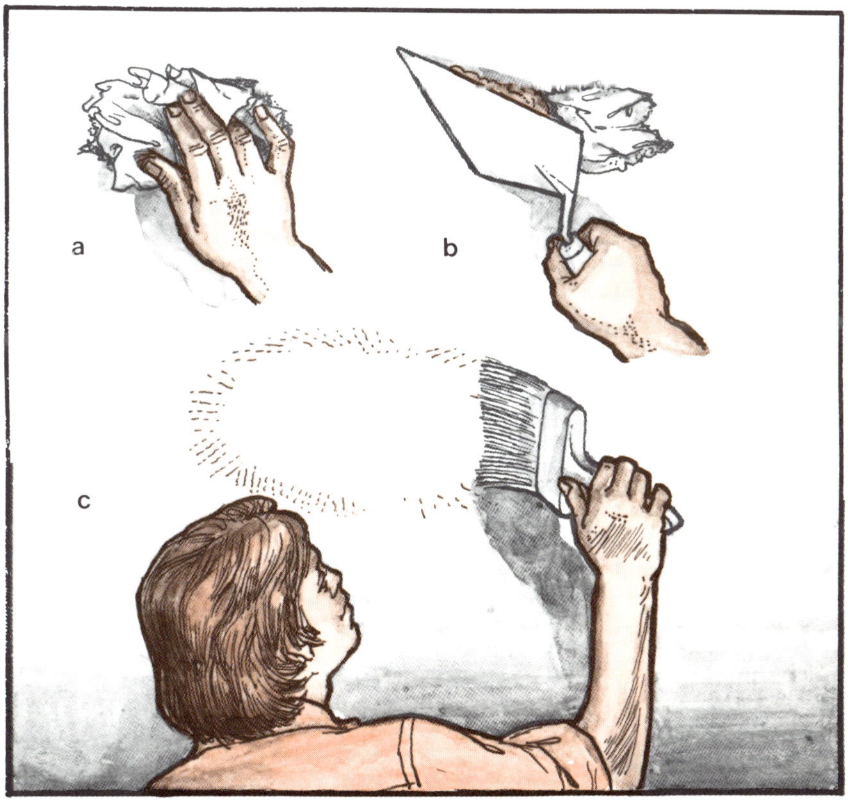

For damaged areas in lath and plaster ceilings (see next page), brush away all dust and push in paper backing, if it is needed, leaving a space of $\frac{1}{4}$in. for the plaster. (a)

Use a trowel to apply the plaster. Leave the first coat slightly below surface level. (b)

Dampen the surface with fresh water before applying the final coat of plaster – or cellulose filler if you prefer. Brush lightly over the repaired area with water to feather out the edges. (c)

LATH AND PLASTER CEILINGS

Small holes in a lath and plaster ceiling can be repaired with cellulose filler or plaster applied directly to the laths.

A large hole, say 3in. wide, should be plugged with stiff, dampened paper or expanded metal nailed to the laths. This will provide a backing for the new plaster.

Expanded metal is a fine metal mesh in sheet form which can easily be cut to size with snips.

FIXING A CEILING COVE

Cracks which appear along the ceiling-to-wall angle are caused by normal house movement. No matter how often these are filled they are almost bound to re-open again.

The permanent answer is to hide them behind ceiling cove.

Blue Hawk cove is 4in. wide and 6ft. long and is fixed with special adhesive.

Corners have to be mitred. These are easy to cut with a fine tooth saw, using a template supplied by the makers.

The special adhesive is mixed to a creamy consistency according to instructions supplied. Only mix the amount you can use in 30 minutes or it will dry out.

After fixing, the cove can be painted.

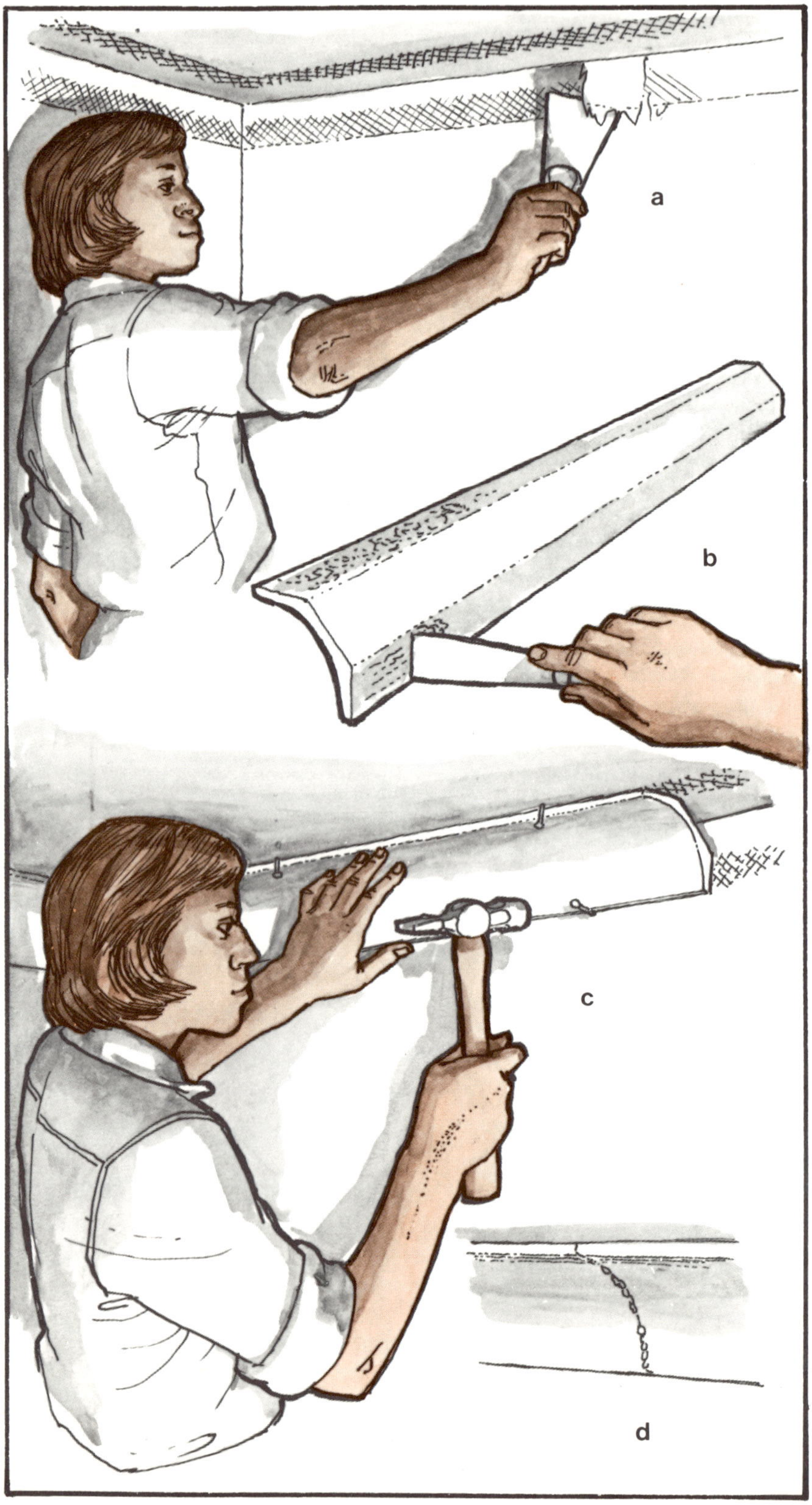

Draw pencil guide lines along the wall and ceiling $2\frac{5}{8}$in. away from the angle. Remove any wallpaper, flaking paint or dust from within the lines. Scratch the area to provide a key for the adhesive. (a)

Butter the adhesive on to the back of the cover. (b)

Push the cove into position. If the adhesive does not take immediately, knock a couple of nails to act as a temporary support. (c)

Make good the joints between lengths with adhesive. Use enough so that it squelches to the surface. (d)

Floors

Dependent on the type of house you have, and its age, you will encounter either wood or solid floors. Pre-war houses will probably have wooden floors; those built after 1945 could have solid floors, though there is no hard and fast rule.

Normally repairs are essential to prevent undue wear to floorcovering material.

Wood floors are comprised of floor-boards, either those which simply butt up to each other, or the more modern types called tongued and grooved. The latter interlock by means of thin strips of timber on one edge which slot into matching gaps in the edges of neighbouring boards.

The boards are supported on joists which run at right angles to them and are, in the ground floor of a house, supported on low walls called sleepers. The sleepers have gaps in them to allow air to circulate freely beneath the timber, thereby preventing damp. This system is called a hollow timber floor.

Tongued and grooved boards are far the best, since even if movement has caused the boards to come apart a little, the projecting tongues will still be partly in the grooves, preventing dust from rising up to the surface.

If you want to find out which type of boards you have and they are still fairly tight together, then force a thin knife blade down into the gap at several points along the length of two adjoining boards. If the blade meets an obstacle, they are tongued and grooved. If it pushes down a way or all the way, they are the butt edge type. You need to know this should you have to remove a board. There is a different technique for removing each type.

When confronted with bare boards, perhaps before laying a carpet, you can make a detailed examination to find spots that may need attention.

The first thing to do is to look for any nails protruding from the floor. Nail heads can snare the backing of a covering material so they must either be knocked below the surface or extracted and replaced by countersunk screws.

To sink the heads you need a hammer and a nail punch. A nail punch is a steel pencil-like tool. Place the tip on the nail head and tap the other end with the hammer.

If a nail is in crooked or it won't sink down for any reason, then remove it with a claw hammer or pincers and replace it with a fresh nail. In upstairs rooms where hammering may damage the ceiling below, it is better to use screws.

Drill a starter hole for the screw to avoid splitting the wood as the screw goes in.

A squeak can be caused by two boards rubbing together. A simple, cheap remedy which often works is to puff some talcum powder down between the edges.

A loose screw can cause a squeak. Find the squeaking area, knock in some floor brads and then drive a couple of woodscrews through the board and into the joist below. The positions of nail heads indicate where the joists are located beneath the boards. As an

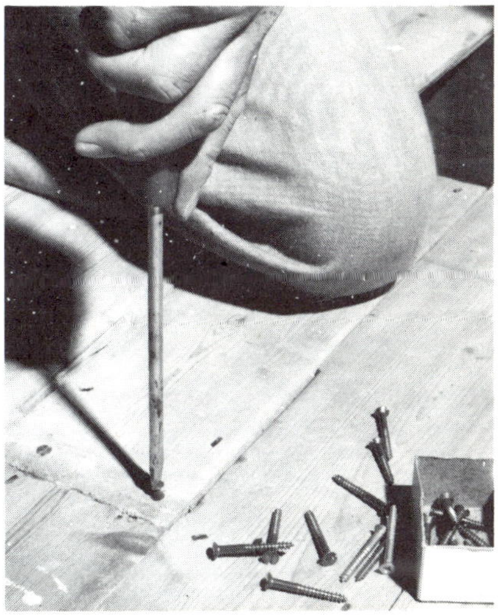

Remove crooked nails with pincers or a claw hammer. In upstairs rooms it is preferable to use screws to re-secure the boards. Hammering can damage the ceiling plaster below.

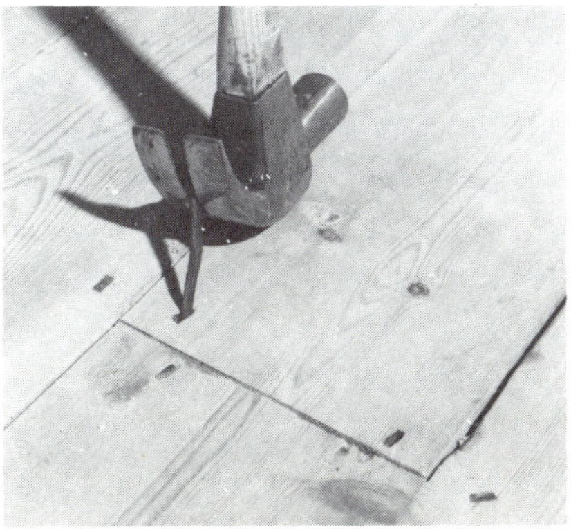

Protruding nail heads can tear into the back of the floorcovering, so they must either be removed and replaced by countersunk screws or else be punched below the surface, using a nail punch and hammer.

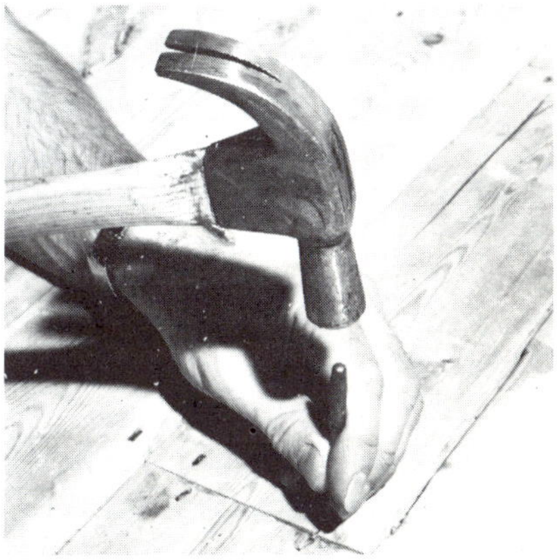

The next most obvious fault is boards which have shrunk apart leaving gaps between them. Even if the gap is still actually sealed by the subsurface tongue, it may be quite wide on the surface and could cause wear of floor coverings. So it is important to remedy the situation and in any case the boards could move again in the future and the gap could widen.

Small gaps need cost practically nothing to repair if papier mâche is used as a filler.

To make papier mâche get plenty of newspapers and soak them in water until they are soggy.

Tear them into small pieces and then squeeze them until all the moisture is drained out. To this raw material, add some glue size. Mix up a stronger solution than directed on the packet for its normal use in preparing walls for wall papering. Dip the newspaper pulp into the mixture and mould the lot together keeping it on the dry side.

Using an old knife, press the papier mâche into the gaps between the floor boards, forcing it well down until the gaps are filled. Leave it to dry out for a while and then sand it flush with the adjacent boards, working in the direction of the grain. This is a quick and cheap remedy for an all-too-familiar floorboard fault.

Wider gaps between boards need different treatment since the papier mâche would just fall through the gap between butted boards. Provided there are not too many gaps, the answer is to fill them with wood battens, slightly thicker than the boards. For easy working the maximum length for any batten must not exceed about 3ft. If, therefore, a gap exists along an entire floorboard length, several will be needed.

Cut the batten to length and form it into a wedge shape with a plane. Cover the lower part of the batten with glue and tap it down into the gap until it is a tight fit. Allow plenty of time for it to set before planing down the protruding edge to floor level.

Creaks and squeaks can be very

Use an old knife to press papier mâché into narrow gaps. Force it well down until the gap is sealed. (a)

Allow to dry, then use glasspaper wrapped around a wooden block to sand it flush with adjacent boards. Work in the direction of the grain. (b)

Fill wider gaps with wedge-shaped battens. Apply glue to the lower half of the battens.
Tap the battens into the gap. (c)

Allow the glue to set and then plane the protruding edge flush with the surface. (d)

irritating, but they can simply be a pointer to two boards rubbing together. To find out, walk across the room in all directions, making sure that a good deal of pressure is exerted on all areas until you hear a tell-tale squeak.

If it is boards rubbing together, a simple remedy which can be effective is to puff talcum powder well down between the edges of the boards. This will act as a lubricant and cure the squeak. Failing this, you might have to buy an aerosol of timber lubricant to squirt between the rubbing edges.

Creaks can sometimes be attributed to a loose board. Refixing loose nails or screws might be the answer, so try this first. If it fails, buy some floor brads, about 1½in. longer than the thickness of the boards and hammer them into the loose area, using a nail punch to sink them below surface. Follow up by inserting a couple of woodscrews through the board end into the joist below. Locating the joists is easy. Just find the existing nail heads.

SMOOTHING A LARGE AREA

When floor boards have warped they create an undulating surface that must be levelled off before laying a floorcovering.

A lot of hard work is involved in sanding boards smooth if hand tools are used. Most people would prefer to simplify the job by using an electric floor sanding machine. These can be obtained from hire shops.

Before using a sander, or even a plane, to smooth floorboards make sure that all nail heads are knocked below the surface, using a hammer and nail punch. If you possess a sharp plane this can be used to smooth small areas of floorboards but is very laborious work over a whole floor.

A floor sander works like a vacuum cleaner. An abrasive belt does the work and the dust created is automatically collected in a bag. Even so, this can still be a fairly dirty operation so keep the door of the room shut and open windows for ventilation.

Ask for a selection of abrasive sheets at the hire shop. These are fitted in sequence. A coarse grade is used for the initial work, the medium grade is needed to give a smooth finish and the final 'sweep' is made with a fine grade abrasive.

With a coarse grade abrasive belt fitted to a floor sander, work diagonally across the room.
When using a medium or fine grade abrasive, work in the direction of the boards.
The sander will not reach into corners, so use a sanding disc fitted to an electric drill.

REPLACING FLOORBOARDS

When a floorboard is in such a poor state that replacement is the only sensible solution, think carefully and shop around before buying new timber. Floorboards are an expensive item – timber prices being what they are today – and since you might not be able to buy timber to match the thickness of the existing boards, go for something a fraction thicker and trim back with a plane when the board is in position with the nails driven well below the surface. The older type of boards can be removed with a bolster chisel and a club hammer. Remember, however, to turn off the electricity at the mains before you start work. Electric cables and water pipes run under floorboards so work with great care until you can see what may be there. Since economy is important when using timber, it may be possible only to replace part of a board.

Here, locate the joist nearest to where the board is to be cut and mark a cut line in pencil just in front of the nails.

Sawing through floorboards in situ is impossible with an ordinary hand saw. The ideal tool to use is a pad saw which has a very thin blade and can be operated in restricted areas. But even for the pad saw, you have to make a starter hole into which the blade can be inserted. Do this by drilling two or three holes closely together to form one big one.

When you have sawn across the width of the board, insert a bolster chisel into the cut and prise up the end. Push a batten under the raised end to keep it up before sawing through the board immediately on top of the joist at the other end. It can then be lifted clear.

Support the new piece of board with a small batten screwed firmly to the joist. Use screws to fasten down the new piece of board.

Tongued and grooved boards are more of a problem to remove since you have to saw through the tongues first before prising up the board.

It is very much a professional's job to lay a complete tongued and grooved floor and there are, anyway, some ideal and much simpler alternatives.

When faults in boards extend over a wide area, it really is not worth your while to attempt repair. The same thing applies where you encounter other faults such as extensive woodworm or rot bad enough to mean extensive replacement.

Where damage is confined to wear and tear, you can lay a new surface of hardboard sheets. Hardboard is bought in 8ft. × 4ft. sheets and, for this purpose, should be sawn into 4ft. × 2ft. panels.

The sheets have to be conditioned to the room's atmosphere before laying. This involves damping the sheets with water – two pints to an 8ft. × 4ft. sheet is the usual amount.

To replace part of a board, draw a line across the board in front of the nails securing it to the joist.
Make a starter hole for a pad saw by drilling three holes closely together to form a gap big enough for the saw to operate. (a)
The thin blade of the pad saw is essential for working in restricted areas such as this. (b)

Keep the cut end raised with a batten. It may be necessary to prise up the cut end with a bolster chisel to tap in the batten. Saw through the other end of the board immediately on top of the joist. Then lift the board clear. (c)

Screw a batten to the joist to support the new piece of timber. Fix the new board with screws. (d)

For tongue and grooved boards, drill starter holes for the saw and cut along the tongue before prising it up with a bolster chisel. (e)

As if dealing with a butt-edged board, lever it out in the same way, after removing the nails or screws holding it to the joists. (f)

Lay the hardboard in the room where it is to be used for 48 hours before fixing. Use hardboard nails to secure the sheets and stagger all joining edges. And, as always, punch the nail heads below surface.

LAYING A NEW SURFACE

Where complete removal of the boards is necessary, a new surface can still be formed quite easily by laying chipboard sheets over the joists. The chipboard must be 18mm. flooring grade. It is simply a matter of cutting out the sheets to coincide with the formation of the joists and ensuring that all edges are well supported.

Fix the chipboard to the joists with 2in. screws inserted no more than 1ft. apart. Where necessary, perhaps in an awkward corner, fix battens to the joists as supports for the edges of the chipboard. And remember, that access to underfloor wiring or pipes will still be needed, so cut inspection panels in appropriate places that can be removed quickly when necessary.

SOLID FLOORS

And now for solid floors. Problems here are likely only to be slight. Cracks, possibly undulations, will be the only faults.

The simple solution is to cover the whole floor with a screeding compound. Special self levelling types are available from d-i-y shops. You simply mix the powder with water according to the manufacturers instructions and spread it over the affected area with a stiff broom, and smooth it roughly with a trowel, leave it to dry and it will set perfectly level.

STAIRS

Stairs are notorious for squeaks. The problem here is usually found in loose wooden wedges which hold the risers and treads in place. They can shrink, crack or work loose.

For creaking stairs, remove any defective wedges, apply adhesive and tap them firmly back into place. If a wedge has shrunk too much, make a new one. (a)

It is not always possible to get under the stairs, of course. Here, a couple of screws driven through the squeaky treads into the risers will usually cure the problem. (b)

If a carriage block works loose, refit it with pins and glue. If the block remains a loose fit, cut a new one from softwood. (c)

Alternatively, screw angle brackets in position. The arm must be a little shorter than the steps. (d)

SKIRTINGS

Skirting boards take a constant pounding from vacuum cleaners, toys, furniture and anything else likely to come into contact with them. As a result they quickly become chipped, cracked and generally an eyesore.

If you have to replace a skirting and you prefer conventional ones made of timber, you can get replacement lengths from builders' merchants or timber yards. Where these skirtings meet at corners, the ends have to be mitred to give a neat join. Skirtings with ready mitred ends can be bought and it is advisable to get this type since cutting neat mitres is not an easy job.

You might, however, decide to opt for making your own maintenance-free skirtings from chipboard or plywood faced with laminate.

Skirtings are fixed by nailing them to wood battens or plugs set in the walls.

Use a claw hammer or a crowbar to prise the skirting away from the wall. To prevent damage to the plaster above, interpose a timber batten between the hammer and the wall.

To help locate the positions of fixing plugs after the new skirtings are positioned over them, mark their positions on the floor.

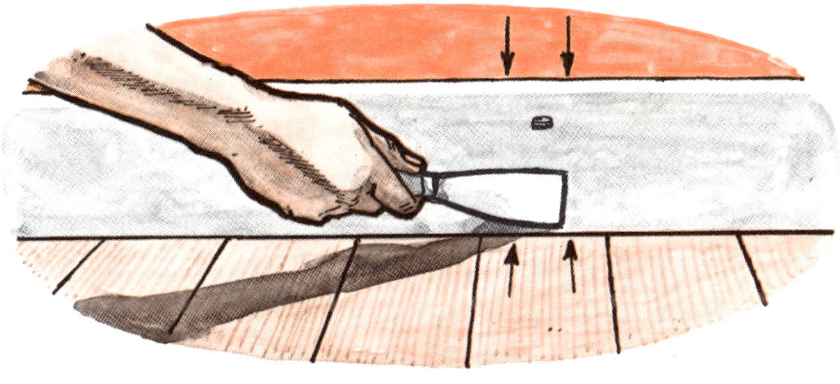

Fit new timber skirtings by driving nails into the existing plugs. Sink the nail heads below the surface and fill the holes with wood filler before painting.

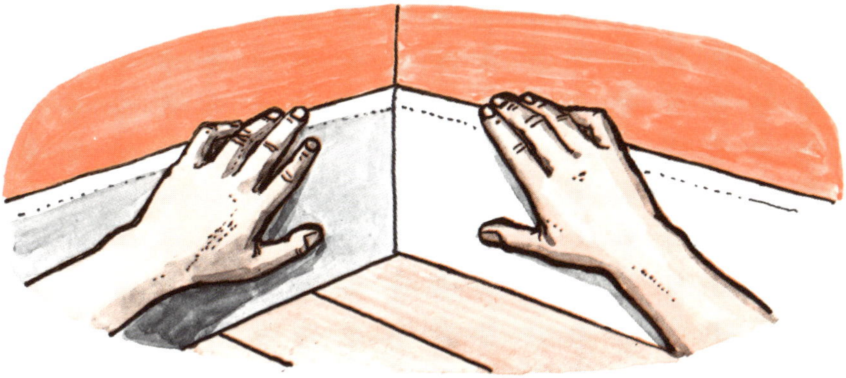

Butt the mitred corners closely together before nailing.

To cut mitres, use a mitre block. (a)

To cut internal corner pieces accurately, temporarily nail one piece in position and mark on it the profile of the skirting on the return wall. (b)

Remove the timber from the wall and cut along the pencil line, using a panel saw. (c)

The cut piece will then meet the other skirting to provide a neat fit. (d)

For blockboard or plywood skirtings use nails or screws to fix lengths of blockboard or plywood to the existing wood plugs. Sink all screw or nail heads below the surface. When possible, the top edge or lipping should be applied and trimmed before fixing the lengths to the wall.

Fix the laminate facings in position (see page 13). Then trim back with a file when the lengths are on the wall. This provides a concealed fixing.

Being thin, quadrant moulding is flexible enough to be able to follow any slight unevenness in the boards and hide it.

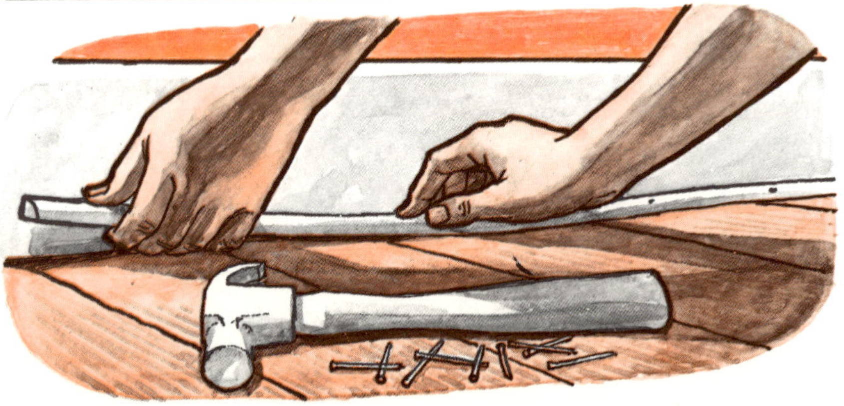

Uneven floors Where a floor is uneven, an ugly gap will be left at intervals between the bottom of the skirting and the floorboards.

Two choices are open to you here. The simplest solution is to fit the skirting board and then conceal the gap by nailing quadrant moulding to the skirting.

The alternative is to cut the skirting to match the shape of the floor.

The alternative is to pin the skirting in position; checking with a spirit level that it is horizontal.

Cut a block of wood that is a little thicker than the widest gap between the skirting and the floor.

Run the block along the skirting, following its path with a pencil.

Cut along the pencil line with a saw and the skirting should fit perfectly. Remember that if the skirting is fixed $\frac{1}{4}$in. clear from the floor, a fitted carpet can be tucked under it.

Roof Repairs

The most important aspect of working at a height is safety. The essential thing before attempting any roof repairs is to get the proper equipment and secure it correctly before using it.

A ladder must extend at least three rungs above the level of the eaves. From there, you will need a roof ladder or a duckboard which spans the distance between the eaves and the ridge of the roof. This equipment can usually be hired locally. Ask your supplier for specific instructions on fixing the duckboard or roof ladder securely to both the ridge and to the main ladder. If you feel unsafe at height then get professional help. The use of ladders and scaffolding is covered in detail in a later chapter.

Many people wait until the roof gives trouble before attempting a repair. This is a bad policy.

It is essential to make a regular inspection of the roof since a lot of damage can be caused before the tell-tale signs of leaks start to appear on ceilings and walls.

A reasonable overall inspection of the roof can be made from the ground using binoculars, though a close-up examination of suspect areas will then be needed.

Go up into the loft when it is raining heavily and look and listen for any drips or splashes which will indicate cracked or displaced tiles or slates.

Very often the defect will be some distance from where the water is actually dripping. Use a torch to trace the water back to the trouble spot.

Pre-war houses generally have roofs of slates or plain clay tiles. Thereafter roofs were covered with single-lap concrete tiles or plain, triple-lapped concrete tiles. The single-lap tiles interlock with adjacent tiles through tongues and grooves in their sides. There are various types and patterns available.

In plain tiling the roof battens are about 4in. apart. The tiles should overlap by not less than 2½in. They are secured to the battens by two projecting nibs. The tiles in some courses may be nailed, depending on the design of the roof and the tiles used.

TILE ROOF REPAIRS

Old tiles must be replaced if they are crumbling or cracked. To remove a defective tile, lift the edges of adjoining tiles and insert wedges to hold them up while the defective tile is removed.

Where a tile is nailed, a trowel can often be used to lever out the nail holding the tile. If not, you will need a ripper. This tool has a hooked blade. They can usually be hired locally.

Hook the blade around the nail and pull sharply to cut through the nail.

To fit the new tile, push it back until the nibs hook over the battens. It cannot be nailed if the overlapping tiles are not removed.

Some old roofs are covered with nibless tiles nailed to the battens. If a tile slips down, the only remedy is to lift and renail all the tiles in position.

Finding matching replacement single-lap tiles is often difficult. Many of the older patterns are no longer made. Very likely, though, the particular type you want will have been used in a lot of other houses in the area. So hunt around nearby builders' merchants or demolition firms as one may stock some of the type you need. But be careful. Before buying old tiles make sure they are not crumbled or cracked.

If you do locate a source of matching tiles, it would be worth while taking a few extra ones home and storing them in case they are needed in future.

Lift the tiles in the course above the damaged tile. Raise the damaged tile upwards to release the holding nibs from the battens. Slide out the damaged tile.

Wedge up the tiles above and slip the fixing nibs of the new tile over the roof batten to lock it in place. Remove the wedges and lower the tiles above back into place.

SLATE ROOFS

A single slate or two can be replaced quite easily, but a bigger job involving cutting or drilling is best left to a professional.

Slates are brittle and difficult for the amateur to cut to shape or drill through.

Cracks and breaks are the usual problem with slates though the fixing nails can corrode leaving a slate loose.

Slate tiles can be bought with predrilled holes either at one end of the slate (mainly for fixing at the ridge of the roof or the eaves) or in the centre (for slates fixed elsewhere). Always replace a slate in the same way as it was fixed before.

They are nailed to battens in the roof in such a way that a single slate overlaps two in the row below.

Various slate sizes are in common use and some types are thicker than others.

A special tool called a ripper will be needed to remove damaged slates.

If a slate slips because the fixing nails have corroded, it can be re-fixed with a strip of lead, zinc or aluminium, 1in. wide or, alternatively, heavy gauge copper wire nailed to the batten through the slight gap between the pair of slatcs below.

The new slate is pushed into position and the projecting end of the clip is turned up and over to grip the tail of the slate.

If they are sound, there is no reason why old slates should not be used again,

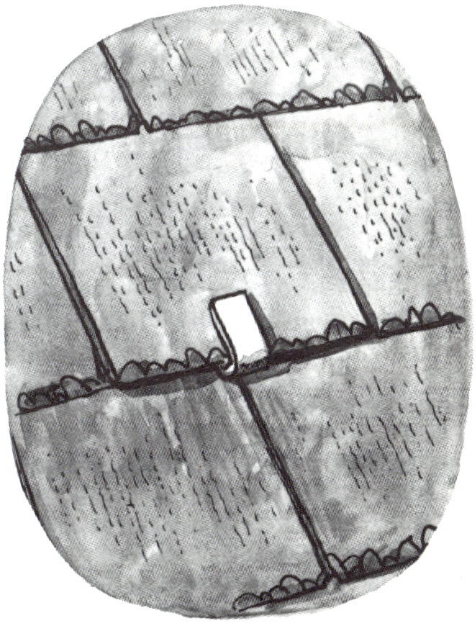

Slide the ripper under the broken slate so that its end locks on to the slate's fixing nails.

Pull or tap the ripper backwards to break the nails. Slide the broken slate gently out.

Nail a strip of lead, about 1 ft. long, to the batten through the remaining slates.

Slide the new slate into place and curl the lead strip around it to hold it in place.

and stocks of slates recovered from demolished houses are often kept by builders' merchants in the locality. These second-hand slates, because they have been weathered, often make a better colour match than new ones, but examine them for defects before buying. To be sure of getting a good colour match, take the defective one with you to your supplier.

REMOVING MOSS FROM ROOFS

Moss forms easily on many roofs. If simply scraped off it will almost certainly reform. The best way to treat the problem is to scrape the area clean, scrub it thoroughly, and then brush on a good coat of suitable fungicide bought from a hardware shop.

RENEWING FLASHING

The point at which the roof of an extension meets the house wall is usually sealed with mortar, or a strip of zinc or lead which is called the flashing.

Mortar is a poor sealer since it inevitably cracks under normal house movement. You can anticipate and avoid trouble by fixing zinc flashing over the mortar.

Old damaged flashing can be levered out with a cold chisel and hammer and replaced with zinc.

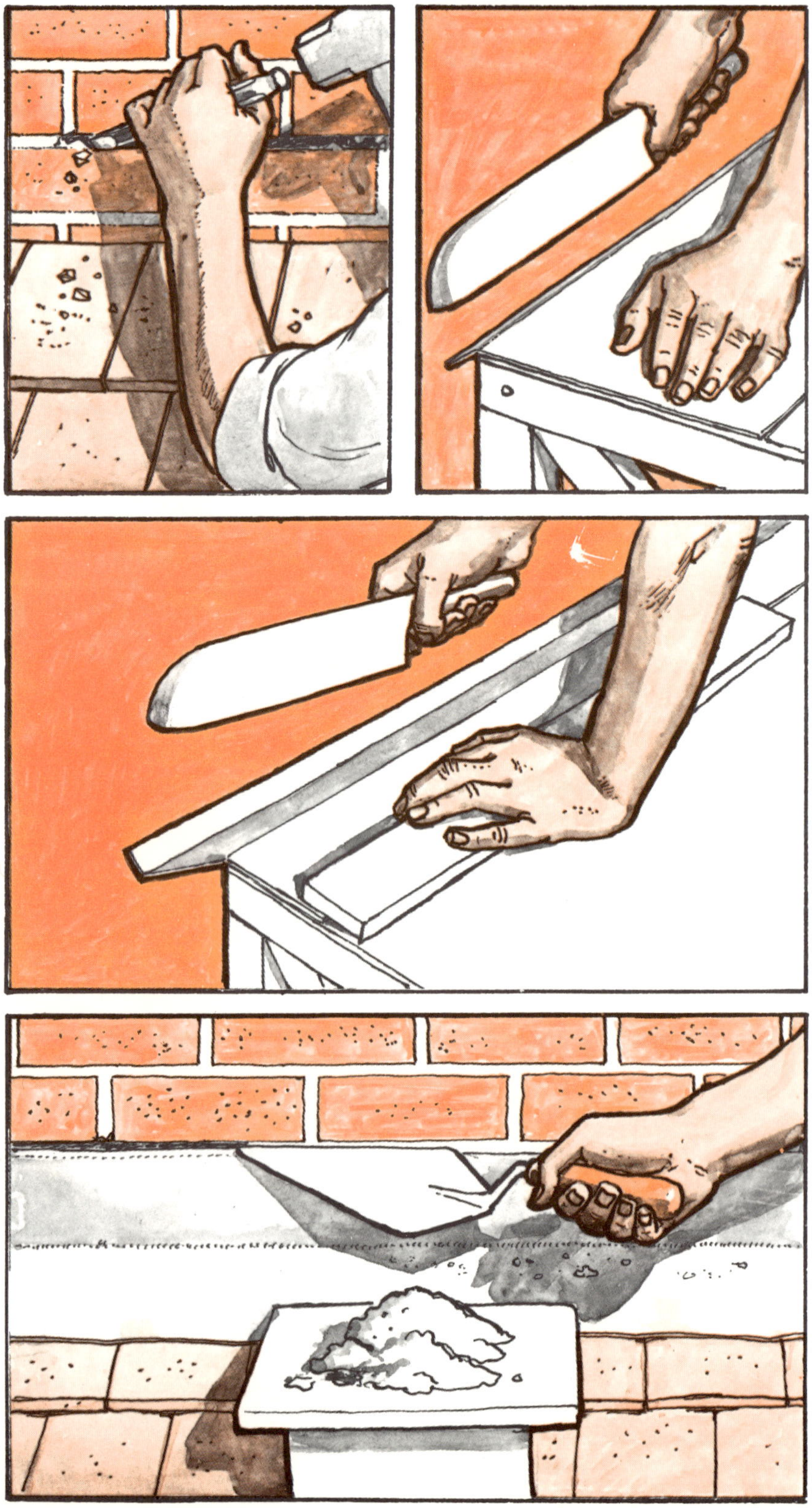

When renewing flashing rake out the mortar from the joint in the brickwork above the roof. Clean it out to leave a 1in. deep cavity.

Use the dresser to form a $\frac{3}{4}$in. wide edge at right angles on the strip of zinc.

Hammer down the other side to suit the angle between the roof and the wall.

Wet the cleaned-out mortar cavity with clean water before slotting the flashing into place. Wedge it in place and fill the joint with a mix of 4 parts sand to one part cement.

A builders' merchant will supply a flat piece of zinc for you to shape to the contours of the roof and wall. They might, however, be prepared to shape the zinc as required if you give them detailed instructions.

If not, you will need to hire a special wooden tool called a dresser. This will enable you to beat the zinc into shape. Ask for the zinc to be supplied in 1ft. wide strips cut to the required lengths. Normally each strip will be 8ft. long.

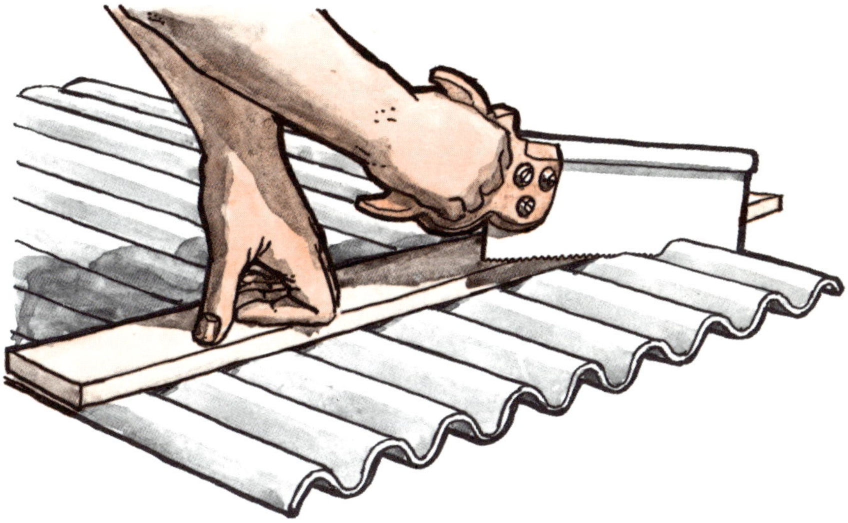

CORRUGATED ROOFS

Older corrugated garage roofs are often made of iron which is a difficult material to cut to size. But a sound repair can be made quite easily with asbestos or Novolux plastic sheet.

If necessary, raise the flashing between the roof (of an attached garage) and the wall by bending it upwards temporarily to free the existing corrugated material.

If you use Novolux plastic sheet, buy the special fixing screws and washers at the same time. Asbestos, an alternative, is fixed with screw nails.

Drill all holes through the raised corrugations of the sheet before inserting the screws.

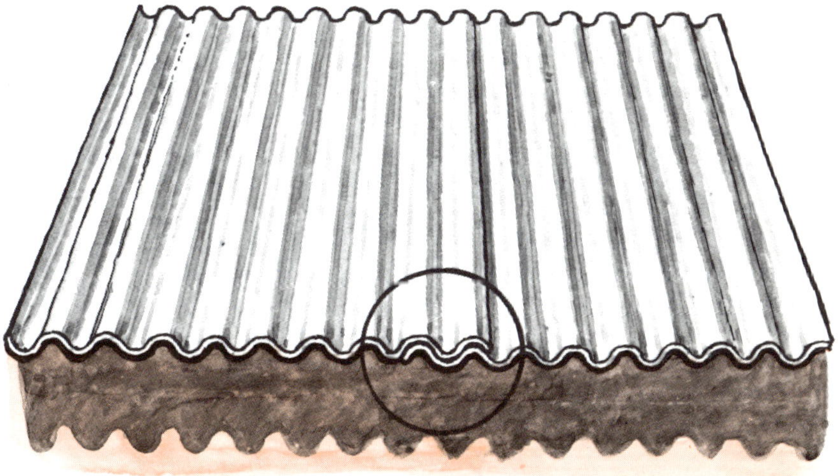

Cut through the raised corrugations, and then reverse the sheet and complete cutting from the other side. A wood batten can be used to guide the saw cut. Saw through the raised corrugations when cutting lengthwise.

Overlap sections by at least two corrugations.

Insert fixing screws through the raised corrugations into the roof battens.

Gutters and Downpipes

The house gutters are fixed to the fascias and connected to the downpipes. Since the gutters are supposed to carry rainwater to the downpipes (from where it goes to the house drainage system) they must be kept in good condition – free of blockages and leaks. A once-a-year check is well worthwhile.

Older gutters were made of metal which can rust away and if you ever have to replace a complete guttering it is worth while changing to the modern plastic types. These will not rust and never need to be painted, though they can leak if a poor joint is made between sections. However, their lightness will make it easier to repair the joint.

Although minor repairs to gutters, or replacing a small length, are within the scope of the average handyman, replacing a whole system is a tricky operation best left to a professional.

Metal gutters are heavy and replacing even a section of these is very much a two-handed job, so get help or once again leave it to a professional.

PREVENTING BLOCKAGES

Trees close to the house will cause leaves to blow into the gutter, so it is a good idea to fit plastic mesh over it to keep out leaves and other debris.

LEAKS

After cleaning a metal gutter, examine the inside for rust spots. Any corroded areas should be cleaned, using a wire hand brush or a wire cup brush fitted to an electric drill.

Coat the cleaned area with a rust inhibiting liquid or with good metal primer.

Repaint with gloss or bituminous paint. If bituminous paint was used before, you cannot use gloss paint over it, because the bitumen will bleed through. A simple test for finding out if it has been used is to apply some white gloss over a small, hidden area. If the existing paint is bituminous, the white gloss will quickly turn brown.

If using gloss paint over old gloss

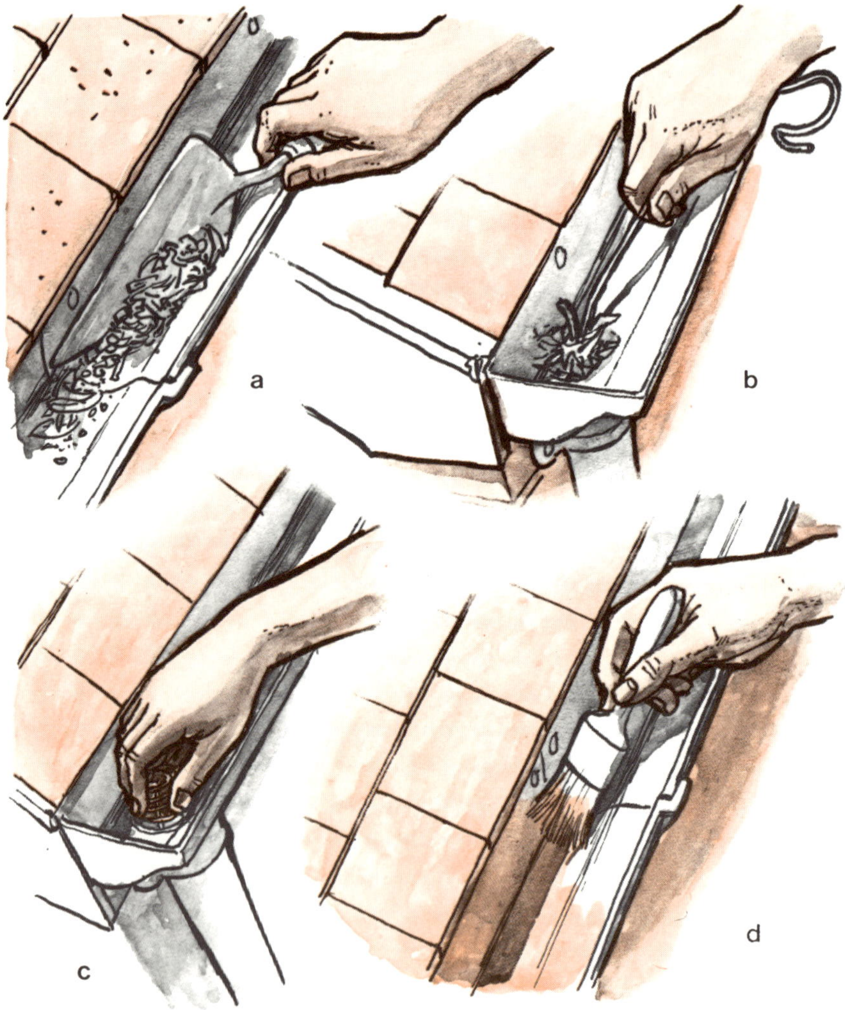

Use a trowel to scrape all leaves and other rubbish from the gutter. Wash out the entire length of the gutter before treating rust spots and priming with metal primer. (a)

Use a piece of stiff wire to lift rubbish from the mouth of downpipes. Birds often nest in the top of a downpipe and sometimes the nest gets washed by rainwater into the pipe. Be careful when hooking a nest out; if it is accidentally pushed further into the pipe it will cause a serious blockage. (b)

Prevent birds building nests on the downpipe by fitting a wire cage to the top. These are simply pressed into position. Get one that is the same diameter as the downpipe. (c)

Minor leaks can sometimes be cured by applying a couple of coats of bitumastic paint after cleaning the affected area. (d)

you can use up old cans of any colour. The colour will not show from the ground since it will be on the inside only.

Cracks and holes must be repaired carefully after cleaning away rust. If holes are large, a new length of gutter will be needed.

Cast iron gutter joints Leaks from the joints of a cast iron gutter means uncoupling the overlapping sections and applying a sealing compound or putty before rejoining the lengths.

DISMANTLING A METAL DRAINPIPE

If a downpipe gets blocked and the obstruction cannot be removed from the top, the downpipe will have to be dismantled and cleaned with a long cane with a cloth pad tied to the end.

Each length of metal downpipe just slots into the section below. Overflowing water at a joint will indicate the position of the blockage. Downpipes retaining brackets are nailed to wooden plugs inserted in the house walls. If a plug has worked loose, it has to be replaced with a larger one.

a

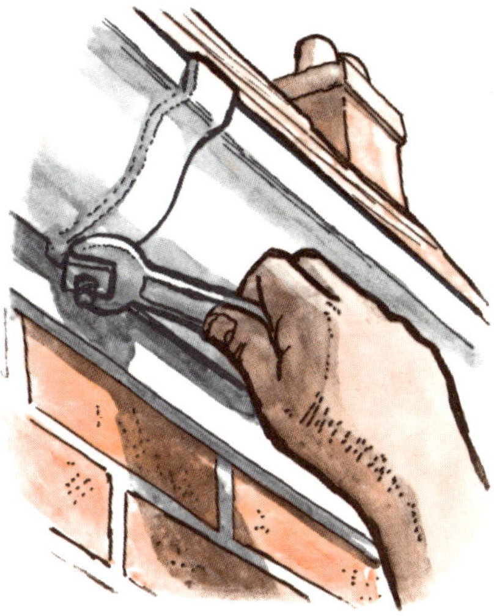

b

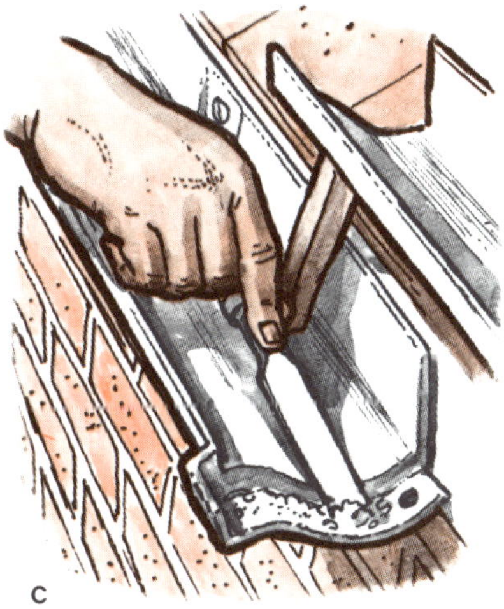

c

d

Fill cracks or holes with bituminous mastic compound or plastic padding. Follow maker's instructions. (a)

The overlapping sections of the gutter are joined by a nut and bolt. Unscrew the bolt and prise the sections apart. (b)

Use an old chisel to scrape away the existing sealing material. Spread a new layer of sealing compound or putty. (c)

Press the two sections together again; tighten the fixing bolt. Trim away the surplus mastic and apply a coat of bituminous paint or a mixture of old left-overs from your gloss paint. (d)

Use a claw hammer to lever out nails from the wood plugs in the walls. (e)

Pull apart the interlocking sections of downpipe and clean them out. (a)

When refitting the downpipe, it may be necessary to cut longer and thicker conical-shape wood plugs to fit tightly into the holes in the wall. (b)

Knock back the securing nails that hold the brackets to the plugs. (c)

If leaves collect around joints, water may settle and turn to ice, eventually splitting the pipe. Seal off any joints between sections with proprietary mastic and apply a coat of bitumen paint. (d)

PLASTIC GUTTER LEAKS

If a joint in a plastic gutter leaks soon after fixing it is most often the result of a poor joint having been made and it must be re-done.

If the leak occurs after the guttering has been in place for a considerable period, then the foam plastic seals on the joining pieces that hold the sections together will have to be replaced. There are several makes of plastic gutters and therefore several types of seal. Make sure you get the right type for your particular gutter system.

Free the joining piece between sections by squeezing its front edge inwards. Remove all traces of the old seal.

Fit the new seal, making sure that the edges of the joining piece are covering its edges.

ALIGNING A GUTTER

In order that rainwater can flow into the downpipes, gutters have to be set at a slight slope. This can vary according to individual systems so check first with the manufacturers of the system you have before attempting installation or repair work. The minimum fall is usually 1in. in 10ft.

If water overflows at the centre of a gutter which is already installed, check that the fall is correct. If the trouble is due to a broken or loose bracket causing the gutter to sag in the middle, this can easily be refixed.

If the fault extends along the complete length the whole system will have to be taken down and re-positioned. This is really a job for an expert.

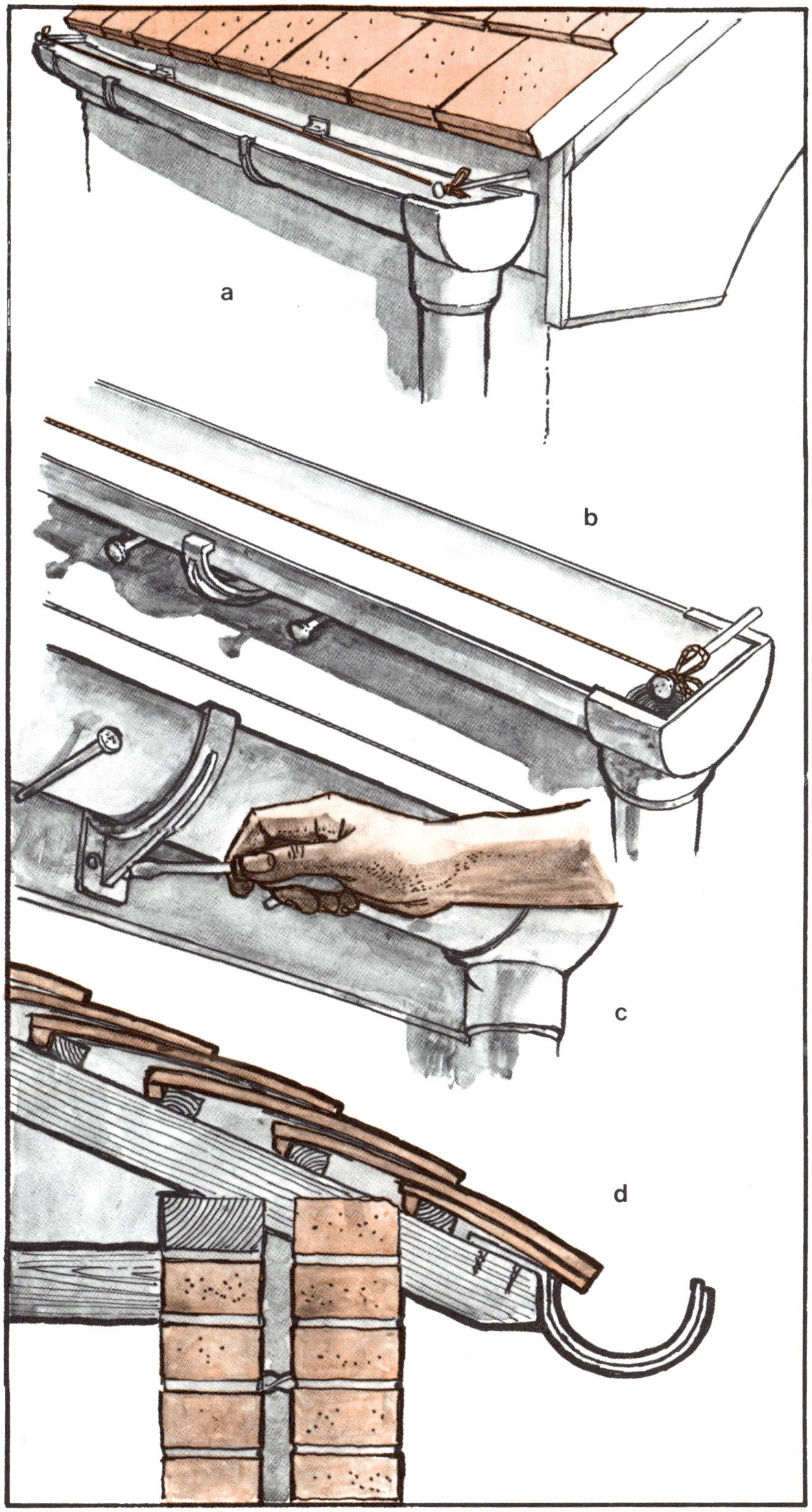

To correct a slightly sagging gutter, first stretch a taut string line along the top of the gutter. Check with a spirit level that the gutter falls evenly to the downpipe. (a)

Before removing bracket screws, knock a couple of nails into the fascia to support the gutter temporarily in its new position. (b)

Insert the screws through the brackets in their new positions. The temporary nails and the string line can now be removed. (c)

If the bracket is fixed to the rafters, a tile has to be removed to reach the old bracket and to refix the new one (see page 46). (d)

Rust

Rust can have a devastating effect on metalwork. Removing it is a really painstaking and time consuming job. The best approach to the rust problem is to put all your efforts into preventing it. The time and money needed is negligible compared to that required for its removal.

Iron and steel are the metals prone to rust attack. These are the ferrous metals which, in their original state, are iron oxide. Rust is the outward sign of them trying to return to their natural state.

Water, oxygen and carbon dioxide, combining to attack the metal, causes the corrosion. The electric potentials of varying parts of the metal differ during the attack and when moisture (rainwater, for example) bridges the parts, currents flow between the negative and positive areas. A chemical change takes place in parts of the metal which is seen as rust.

Assuming then, that prevention is the best cure, what can be done?

Paint is often assumed to be a complete protection against rust; this is not so. Extra paint coats will simply make it more difficult for moisture vapour to penetrate through to the metal surface. They do not keep it out all together.

Even tiny cracks in the paint surface are an open invitation to rust so regular checks are essential on exterior metalwork to make sure that the paint film is unbroken on all surfaces.

If any cracks in the paint are spotted, deal with them immediately.

Not all exterior metal surfaces are painted however. Where this is so, and where damp is likely to be encountered, apply a liberal coat of grease or oil. Hard-to-reach areas can be treated with a film of water-displacing fluid available from builders' merchants.

Garden tools At the end of the summer, it is traditional to put all the tools and gardening equipment into storage – often in the shed at the bottom of the garden. In an uninsulated shed without any form of continuous, even heat, rust attack is likely.

If possible, bring all metal equipment into the house during the winter. If tools have to be stored in a shed, put them in drawers or boxes allowing just a little air to infiltrate. A thorough coating of grease on all the metal parts is essential. Check the equipment during the winter and repeat the greasing treatment. Specially impregnated rust inhibiting paper for wrapping them in is available that will keep the corrosion at bay for a good while.

Cars The family car is one of the most likely targets for attacks from corrosion. The chassis and underside are most prone to attack and even if the car is garaged, it is no protection.

Ideally when the car is new, the underside should be protected with underseal and this is a wise investment, provided it is done immediately.

If this was not done – or the car was bought second-hand – then check the undersides for rust. Never be deceived by shiny bodywork – this is no indication as to what is going on underneath.

Hose down the underside of the car to remove all caked mud and grime. Then spray the whole area with moisture displacing oils. A hosing down is important too after a snowy spell.

When the authorities spread salt on the roads, this is inevitably thrown up on to the underside of the car and will cause corrosion if it is not washed off.

WATER TANKS

Because the domestic water tank is tucked away out of sight in the loft it is often ignored – until it is too late and corrosion has started. Certainly, if it is an older type it will be galvanized and will corrode in time.

A simple protection is to suspend a sacrificial anode into the water. The anode wastes away instead of the galvanizing on the tank. It is also worth while draining the tank and applying a couple of coats of bitumen paint. This colourless, taintless paint will provide excellent protection over a number of years.

But what if, after draining the tank of water, it is found to be hopelessly corroded? Well, in one way, you have been lucky in finding this out in time. Had the tank finally burst, an awful lot of water would have found its way down into the rooms below.

If the tank is beyond repair – that is, the corrosion is severe – there is no alternative but to replace it, but get a plumber to do this.

As a replacement it is best nowadays to buy a polythene type; at least one rust problem will be solved for good.

On the other hand, if the corrosion has only reached the loose, flaking rust stage, this can be dealt with.

Use a wire brush to remove all the

flaking rust. Even better, and less hard work, is to use a wire cup brush fitted to an electric drill. Any minor spots of rust left can be cleaned up with emery paper.

Only attempt to remove the loose rust. The remainder can be painted with a rust inhibiting liquid which will neutralise it to form a hard, inert layer. When dry, this can be painted over.

The alternative is to paint the tank with zinc-base cold galvanizing paint. This kills the rust action and puts an extra layer of zinc on the tank.

RUST REMEDIES

When prevention was overlooked, there is no alternative but to remove the rust as quickly as possible. First of all clean away all signs of rust with one of the methods mentioned earlier.

The metal does not have to gleam but it should be as bright as possible. Use an abrasive paper to rub over the surface.

To dissolve minute particles that are not seen by the eye, use a chemical neutraliser. Immediately apply a coat of one of the pigmented rust-binding metal primers. These compounds neutralise the rust and turn it to iron phosphate, leaving a plastic film on the surface.

When the primer is dry, normal paint can be applied.

RUSTED NUTS AND BOLTS

There are few things more annoying than trying to undo a rusty nut, bolt or a hinge that has locked tight. Dismantling fluid poured on and left for a while usually clears the trouble. This problem can be lessened in future by smearing Vaseline on all screws and bolt threads before inserting.

A screw that has rusted in a wall can sometimes be removed after tightening it a little before unscrewing. If this fails, a soldering iron applied to the screw head can cause sufficient expansion to break the rust grip.

A rusted countersunk screw that will not budge with a screwdriver is really a problem. It cannot be gripped in any way to turn it. However, a twist drill of about the estimated diameter of the screw can be used to drill into the screw head.

Eventually the head will break away and the batten or whatever else the screw is holding in place can then be slipped free and the remaining part of the screw gripped and turned with a suitable wrench.

EXTERIOR METALWORK

Gutters and downpipes can be treated with rust binding primer where the trouble cannot be reached for fuller treatment. Remember that plastic gutters and downpipes are now available and these should be used where existing metal types have to be replaced.

Clean rusty metal window frames with a wire brush followed by emery paper. This should be followed with a coat of rust inhibitor, primer and then the normal paint top coats.

Electricity

An electric current flows, rather like the flow of water in a pipe, but electricity needs a complete circuit to flow round. The flow is measured in amps, it's pressure in volts, and its power (the work it can do) in watts.

Two wires, at least, must be connected to an appliance to provide a circuit. Often there are three, including an earth wire.

If electricity needs a complete circuit for the current to flow, to prevent it flowing when not required, the circuit must be broken. This is the purpose of a switch. A switch turns an appliance on or off, so the circuit is always under control.

A fuse protects the circuit from damage if a fault develops in the wiring, or in an appliance. Like a switch it breaks the circuit and stops the current flowing.

However, unlike the hand operated switch, it works automatically by melting if an excessive current passes through the circuit. When a fuse blows it indicates that something is wrong. Every circuit must have a fuse of the correct rating.

All the electrical fuse boxes and meters and main switches in your home are located in accessible places such as a a cellar, garage, in the hall, under the stairs, or, possibly, in a special meter box outside the house.

The electricity board's service cable brings the electricity supply into your house. It usually contains two wires – live and neutral. Often a terminal is provided on the latter, which is connected to earth and to which all the earth wires in the home are linked.

Your main fuse box contains a fuse which isolates your electrics from the public supply, so if your electrics develop a fault or overload it will not affect anyone else. You must never tamper with this fuse box. It is the property of the electricity board and is sealed.

A meter registers the amount of electricity you have used. The meter

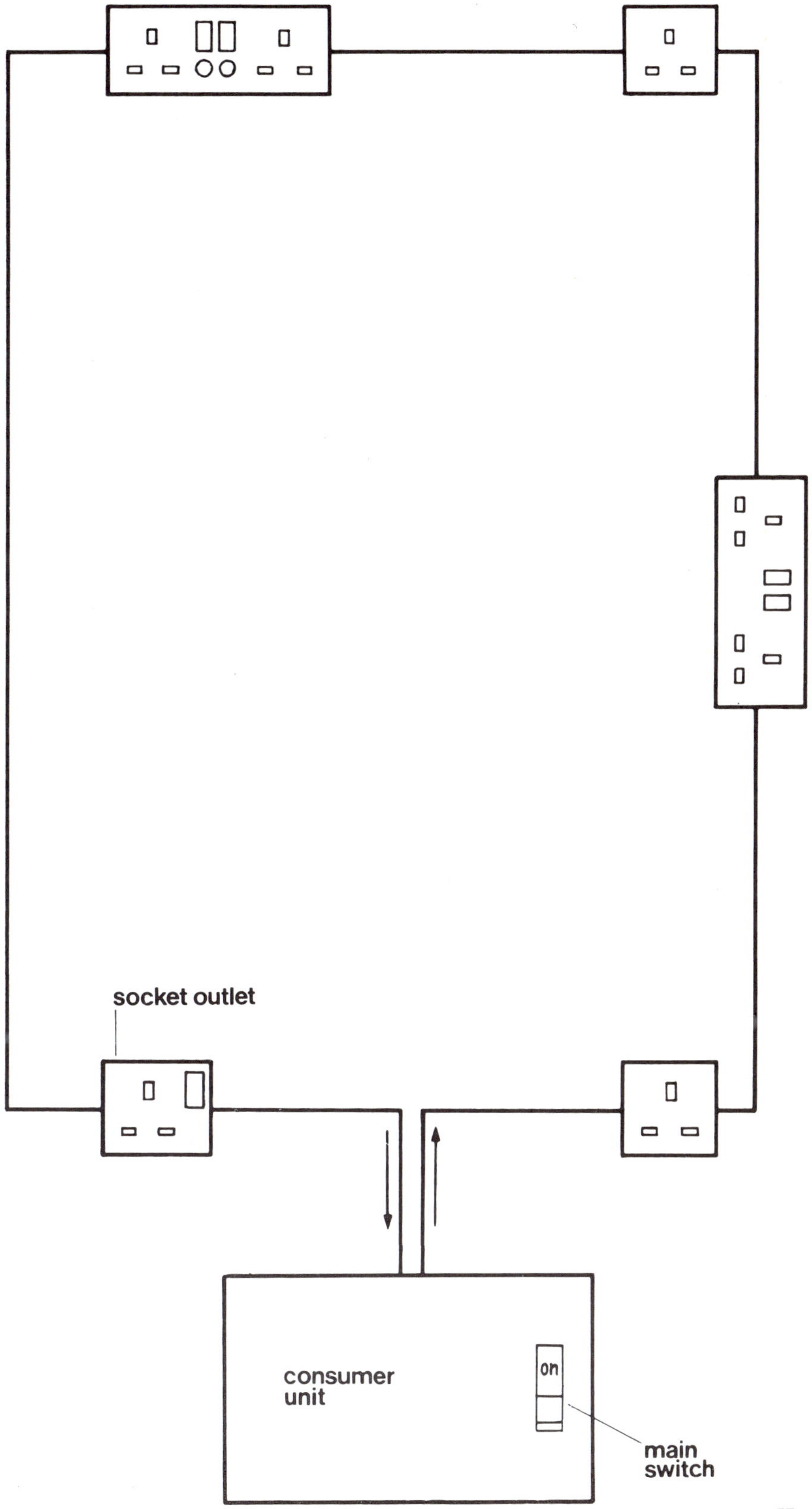

A basic ring circuit.

may be a single black or brown unit, or two meters (one for the cheaper off-peak supply for storage heaters), or a White Meter (for cheaper central heating and hot water). The consumer's installation (the part of the installation which is your responsibility) begins at the meter. It is for you to ensure that the earth connection is effective. A qualified electrician should check the earth connection periodically.

The main circuit in a house is split into a number of sub-circuits by distribution fuses. There is one fuse for each circuit (older installations have two fuses per circuit).

If you have an older-type fuse box ask the electricity board to modify it or install a new one which conforms to modern safety standards.

The cables to separate circuits each contain two supply wires and an earth wire. The cables may be run in tubes embedded in walls, or modern plastic cables can sometimes be embedded without further protection.

The main switch on the circuit fuse box is for switching off the current before replacing a fuse or carrying out any other electrical work. The main switches and fuses should be labelled so that they are immediately identifiable.

The earth connection in the home is for safety. Appliances provided with an earth wire should have the earth wire properly connected. If an appliance is faulty, but properly earthed, the current will take the path of least resistance through the earth wire and not through someone's body to earth. If you touched an unearthed faulty appliance while in contact with a water pipe or water in a bath, or even while standing on a concrete floor or a damp surface, the shock would probably be fatal. You would also get a severe, possibly fatal shock if you touched the bare connections in the plug or a appliance.

COLOUR CODING

Government regulations specify a new colour coding for three-core flexes attached to all new household electrical appliances. These colours have been standardised throughout Europe.

Under the regulations, the earth wire (which was green) is now green with a yellow stripe. The live wire (which was red) is now brown. The neutral wire (which was black) is light blue. Both the old and new types will be in existence for a while so learn the new code as well as the old to avoid making wrong connections.

Cables of wiring systems of old and many new homes will still be red, black and green, so when connecting new flex into permanent connections like a ceiling rose for a light, connect brown to red, blue to black, green/yellow to green (or bare earth wire).

HOW TO WIRE A PLUG

Trim back 2in. of the outer sheath on the flex, without cutting the insulation around individual wires. Push the flex in under the clamp provided in the plug and tighten the clamp on the beginning of the uncut sheath.

Cut the individual wires so that they are just the right length to go through the terminal holes, or around the terminal screws.

Strip off just enough insulation to make the connection and no more. The green or green/yellow is the earth and is connected to the largest pin in the plug – marked E. The red or brown lead is connected to the pin marked L (for live) or R (for Red). And the black or light blue lead is connected to the pin marked N (for Neutral) or B (for Black).

If an appliance has a two-core (two-wire) flex it may be connected to a 3-pin plug as described above, but leaving the larger, earth pin

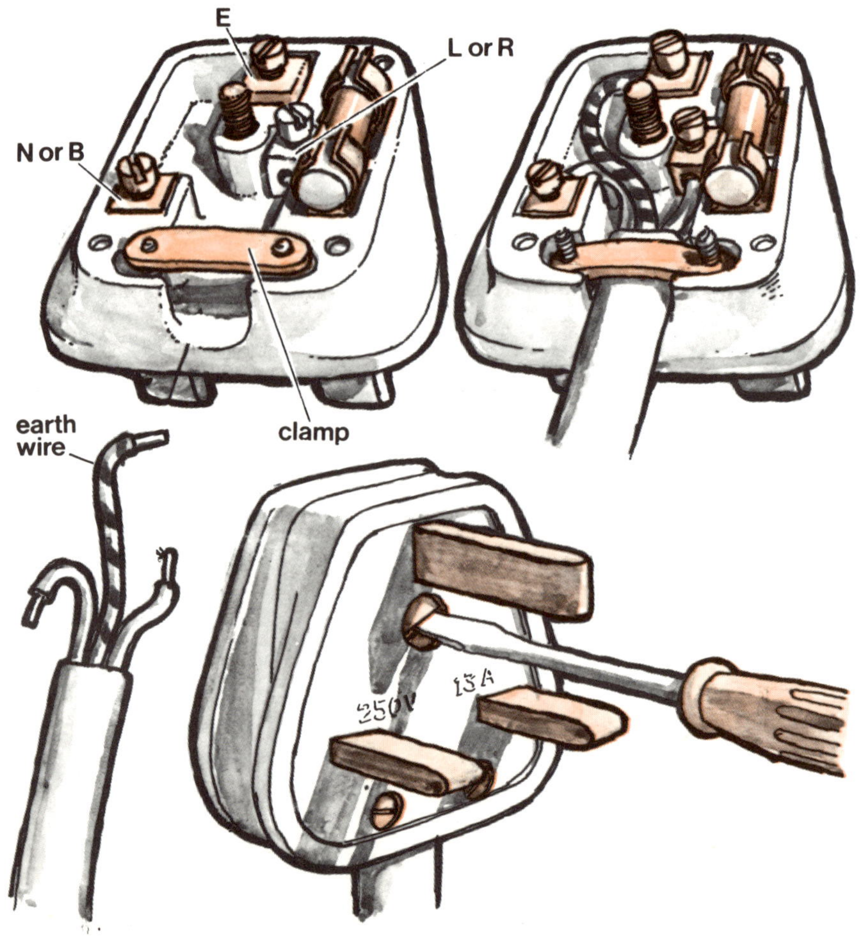

unconnected. Never connect a three-core flex to a two pin plug.

Clamp the wires firmly in the terminal connections.

Before replacing the plug cover, make sure that there are no stray whiskers of bare wire, and that the nuts or screws holding the wires are tight.

Make sure that the outer sheath of flex is secured under the clamp where the lead enters the plug. This will prevent the wires being pulled away from the terminals. Replace the cover and tighten the screws or nuts holding the plug together.

REPLACING AN ELECTRIC FIRE ELEMENT

When an electric fire fails, the usual cause is the element (the bar or bars). Replacing a burnt out element is quite simple but ensure that you replace it with one of the correct type.

First, though, check that the trouble is not more basic. A fuse may have blown or the milled nuts at either end of the element and which hold it in place may be loose. Turn off the fire, unplug it and tighten the nuts.

If this fails you will have to remove the element. First release the guard by removing the retaining screws (if fitted) and squeezing it in the centre to free it from the holes in the casing.

One of the element-retaining brackets has a spring-loaded slot, designed so that, when the nuts are loosened, the element can be eased out.

The reverse procedure is adopted to fit the new element. Push back the spring loaded bracket and locate the fixing pins on either side of the element into the holes in the brackets. Finally, replace the milled nuts and the guard.

WIRING A LAMP HOLDER

Turn off the supply at the mains. Do not just switch off at the light switch.

Unscrew the cap and remove the lampholder.

If the existing flex is in good condition, prepare the ends of the flex by removing about $\frac{1}{4}$ inch of covering.

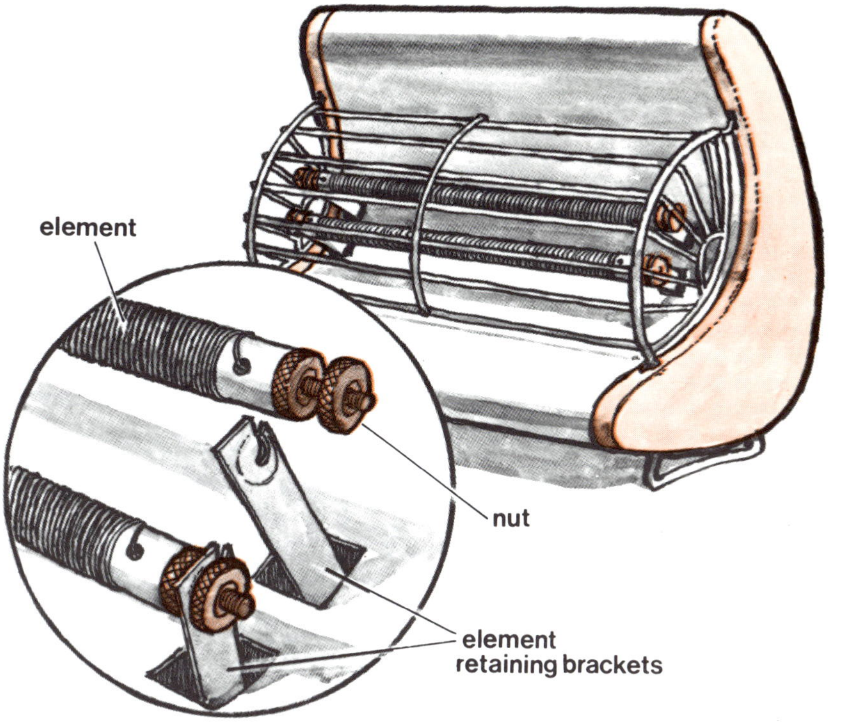

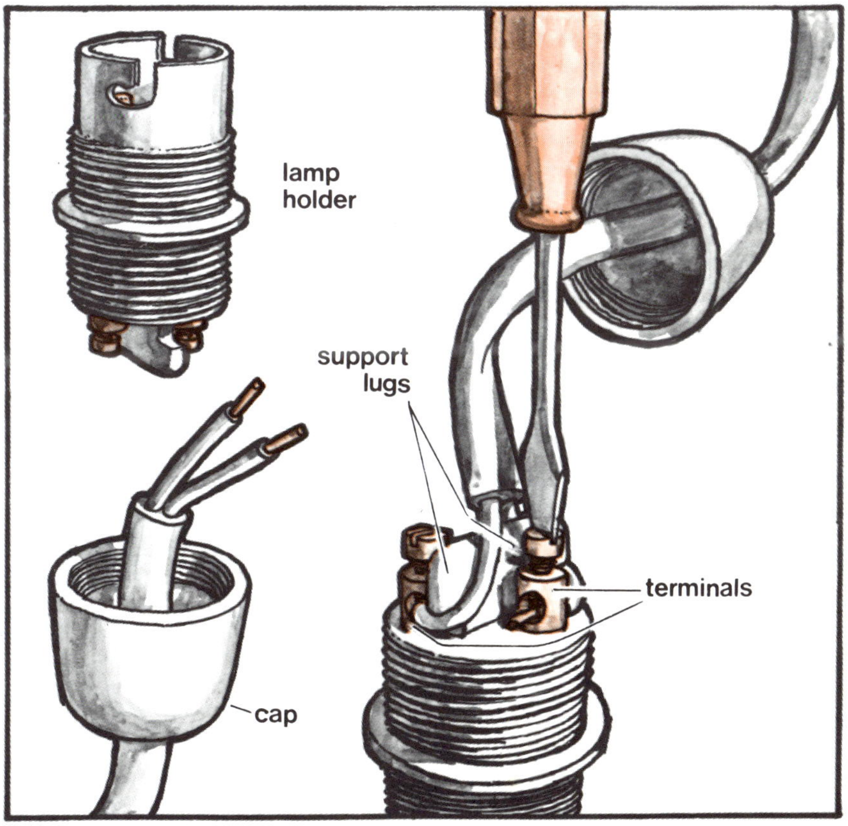

Twist the ends neatly. Use a new piece of flex if the existing flex is frayed, perished or baked hard.

Thread the flex through the lamp-holder cap.

Loosen the small screws in the lampshade terminals, insert the wires, and tighten the screws firmly. Make sure that there are no stray ends of flex spreading out from the terminal.

Hook the flex under the support lugs in the lampholder and screw down the cap firmly. It is important to use the support lugs to avoid straining the connections.

REPLACING A FUSE

Circuit fuses: The usual kind in older installations is the re-wirable type. They are usually rated at 5 amps or 15 amps.

If a fuse blows, turn off the main switch. This may be on the fuse box itself, or possibly in a separate switchbox nearby. Also switch off the faulty appliance or lamp, unplug it, or remove the bulb; otherwise the new fuse might also blow when fitted. Check the wiring of the appliance to see if you can see the fault.

To find the blown fuse take out and inspect each fuse. Usually it is clear which fuse has blown – not only will the fuse wire be broken, but often there will be scorch marks around the fuse carrier.

Replace the old wire with a fresh piece of the correct rating which should be marked on the carrier (a supply of fuse wire should always be kept near the fuse box). Do not stretch or strain the wire when tightening the screws.

Replace the fuse carrier, close the box and then turn on the main switch. If the fuse blows again, or you are in doubt, send for a registered electrician. Get the faulty appliance or light fitting repaired.

Cartridge fuses Your main fuses may be of the cartridge type which are available in different ratings. It is often difficult to find out which one has blown as you cannot see the wire

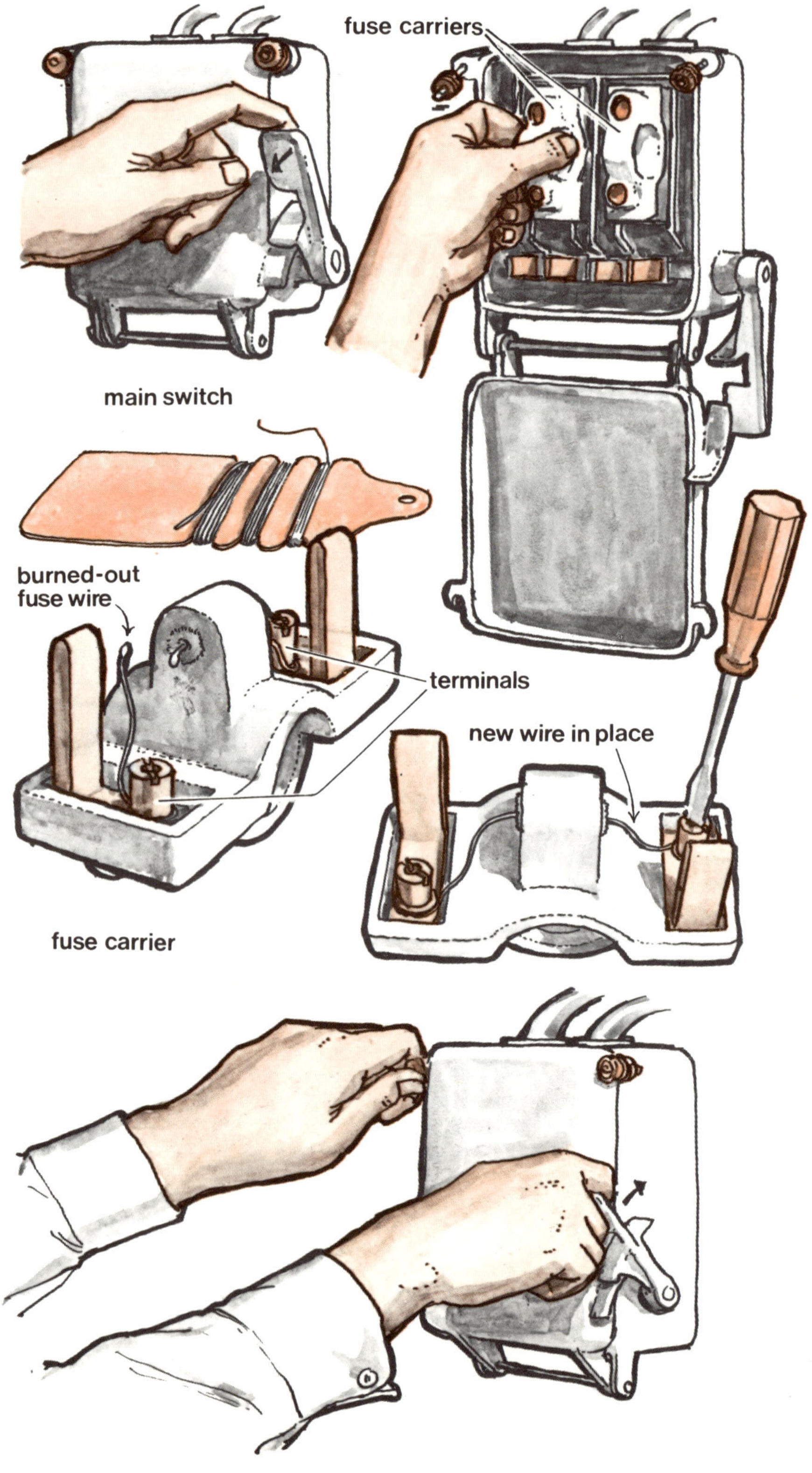

inside, but they are easy to replace.

Turn off the main switch on the fuse box. Try to ascertain the cause of the fuse blowing and take the same precautions as before to prevent it blowing again.

Take out each fuse holder in turn and test the cartridges to see which one has blown. This can be done with the aid of a metal-case torch.

Switch on the torch. Unscrew the bottom cap and place the fuse so that one end touches the metal case of the battery and the other makes contact with the metal of the torch case. If the torch comes on again, the fuse is intact.

If a torch is not available, test by replacing each fuse with another fuse of the same rating.

Replace the fuse carrier, close the box, and switch on the main switch. If the fuse blows again call an electrician. Whenever in doubt get qualified help. Get the faulty appliance or fitting repaired.

Ring Circuit plug fuses Flat pinned plugs contain their own 13 amp cartridge fuses (or 3 amp for appliances rated 700 watts or less).

Always use the correct fuse for the flex. New appliances will be fitted with the correct flex; the watts will be indicated on the maker's rating plate on the appliance and will enable you to select the correct fuse to use.

These fuses are simple to replace – they are located in spring clips inside the plug. Just lever the old fuse out and insert the new one.

It is almost impossible to tell whether a fuse has blown simply by looking at it, but it can be tested with a torch as before.

Appliances with motors – vacuum cleaners and spin dryers, for instance, might need a large fuse even though their rating is less than 700 watts. This is because the starting current required for the motor is higher in the first few moments of running.

SOME THINGS TO REMEMBER

Take good care of flexes. Renew them as soon as they show signs of wear.

Use three pin sockets and plugs where possible, especially in rooms with concrete or tiled floors, or where there is a water supply, or a pipe carrying water.

Never overload a socket by using several appliances from it. It is far better to have a double socket outlet fitted.

Always replace flex with a new unbroken length. Never make joins in a length of flex.

Never secure flex to walls or ceilings without proper conduits or lay it under a carpet.

Never use twisted, unsheathed flex for power appliances.

Never fit socket outlets or take portable appliances into the bathroom.

Bathroom heaters must be out of reach of anyone using the bath as must the essential pullcord switch. Have these installed by a registered electrician.

Try not to knock socket outlets with chair legs or vacuum cleaners. Fixing the sockets a little way up the wall, say 6 inches above floor level, helps to prevent this.

Never touch a fire element until the plug is out and the element is cold.

Never touch a plug, switch or socket with wet hands.

The Electricity Council can be contacted for advice and information on domestic electricity.

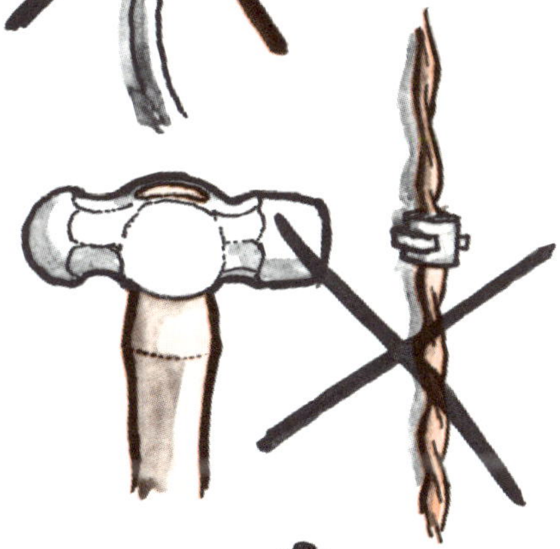

Things you should not do.

Window Maintenance and Repair

How a sash cord works.

Provided that wooden window frames are well looked after they will give a lifetime of service.

A good, sound film of paint is essential at all times. So if the frames are in a poor condition then put matters right now.

Paint will adhere only to a clean, dry surface. If necessary, remove all areas of defective paint and thoroughly clean the bare wood. Slight defects can be overcome by scraping and glasspapering.

Where the paintwork is really rotten, strip it off, using either a blowlamp or chemical stripper and a scraper. Chemical stripper must be throughly washed off and the surface allowed to dry out before painting.

Before using a coat of primer, make sure the bare wood is completely dry. Do not, for example, start work immediately after a rainy spell.

Apply suitable undercoat and finally top coats of gloss according to manufacturer's instructions.

Any gaps between the window frame and the wall can be sealed with a non-hardening mastic which will not shrink. Use a putty knife to work the mastic in to a depth of about ½in.

For added protection, cover the mastic with a small timber moulding fixed with rustless 1in. round nails.

Defective paint spots on steel windows should be scraped, wire brushed, and cleaned with emery paper. Then apply a zinc or aluminium primer followed, as before, with undercoat and top coats.

Eventually, the build-up of paint may prevent proper closing of the window. If so, strip back to bare metal with a blowlamp and scraper before priming and painting again. Protect the glass from direct heat.

If wood casements warp they may bind. Try planing the sticking edge without removing the casement.

Where wood or metal casements are in a really poor condition – beyond simple repair, fix new units. The old windows can be replaced with any suitable modern unit.

Double glazing could be considered if you can afford it. There is more information on double glazing on page 24.

REPLACING SASH CORDS

Older houses often have vertical sliding sashes with balanced weights or cords. These are often in a poor state with worn frames and pulleys and broken or badly worn sash cords.

Broken sash cords are easily removed and replaced by new ones. First, remove the stop bead on the inside (this is pinned in place) and swing out the lower sash.

Remove the parting bead from its groove and swing out the upper sash.

Remove the broad nails which secure the cords in a short groove.

The pocket cover near the bottom of the box frame is normally secured by a screw. Remove the screw and the cover.

Remove the sash cord from its weight after taking it out of the pocket.

Before fitting the replacement cord,

stretch it by looping it round a post and pulling it.

To fit the new cord, tie a string to one end with a nail secured to the free end of the string. Thread the nail and string over the pulley and allow it to drop. It will draw the sash cord down the box frame. Cut the new cord to the same length as the old one and replace the weight in position.

Use galvanized broad-head nails to nail the free end to the sash. Replace the weight, pocket cover and beading.

Exactly the same method is used for the upper sash. The lower sash must be removed first though.

REPLACING OLD WINDOWS

To remove an old timber window frame, cut through the metal lugs, screws or nails holding it to the wall.

Locate these by slipping a thin knife blade between the frame and the wall. Cut through the nail or lug with a padsaw. It may be necessary to chisel away some of the wood to allow the padsaw to gain access to the nail or lug. Remove the frame by striking it with a mallet or by levering it out with a crowbar or similar implement.

To fit a replacement frame, choose a size which is slightly less all round than the 'hole' in the wall.

Manufacturers supply a vast range of standard frames. Their sizes are often in metric measure but usually have imperial equivalents indicated.

The simplest way to fit a new frame is, first, to drive wedges into a mortar joint on the walls on either side of the position of the frame. Obviously the mortar will have to be raked out of the joints first. Soak the wedges in preservative before fitting them and indicate on the brickwork their positions – when the frame is placed in position they will be covered up.

It will probably be necessary to use packing pieces to hold the new frame in place.

Drill through the frames into the wedges so that screws can be inserted to secure the frame.

WINDOW SILLS
Most windows have timber sills of either hardwood or softwood. An unprotected sill will deteriorate rapidly. Softwood will rot and hardwoods (such as oak) which tend to have an open grain will become clogged by dirt and grime.

Paint can only be applied to sound timber.

Scrape or plane off any decayed timber to leave a clean, healthy surface before applying a coat of primer. Any rotten wood must be cut out and, if excessive, fresh timber inserted by gluing and pinning it in place. Then a coat of paint primer can be applied.

Keep the drip groove beneath the sill free from dirt at all times so that rainwater will drain away.

If a sill is really rotten, consider

For making a concrete replacement sill, chisel out the existing sill. Drive in four or five 6in. nails at even spaces into the bottom of the window frame. These should project well into the new sill. They provide reinforcement for the concrete. (a)

Screw a wood batten to the wall to provide anchorage for a timber shutter box in which to place the concrete. The tops of the timber pieces forming the shuttering should correspond with the intended top of the sill. Stretch a line of cord along the base of the shuttering inside the box to form a drip groove. (b)

For the concrete use a mix of 1 part fine shingle, 2 parts clean, sharp sand and 1 part cement. Pack the mix down hard in the shuttering. It should not be too sloppy – aim for a buttery consistency. (c)

When the concrete has set, remove the shuttering and the cord line and then allow to dry thoroughly before painting. (d)

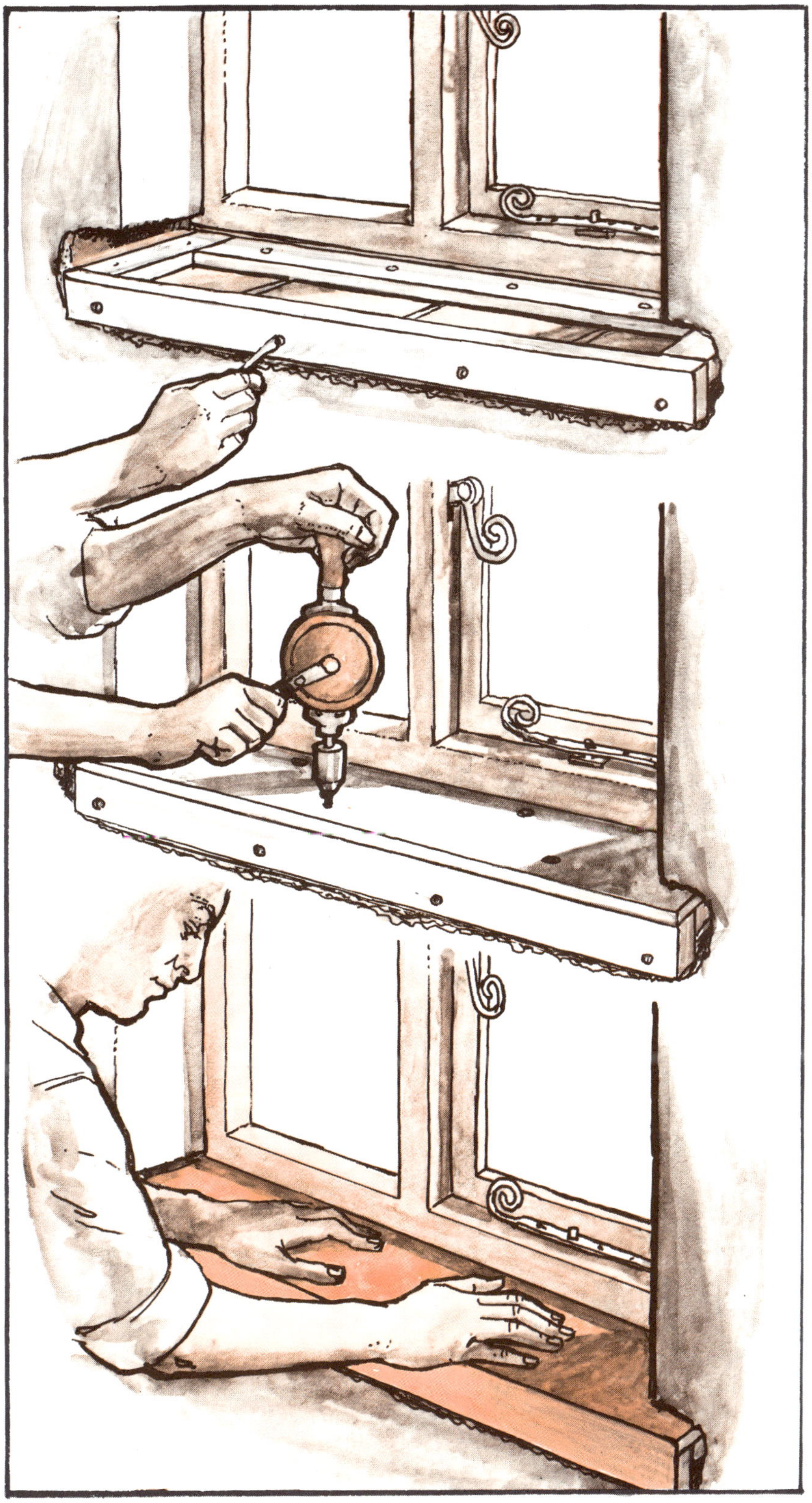

replacing it with concrete. Whereas timber is expensive and sometimes of suspect quality, a concrete sill is economical to construct and will last for many years if properly maintained.

Interior sills Conventional wood painted sills are difficult to maintain at their best. They are constantly being marked by normal household stains from over-filled flower pots, to carelessly placed drinks. They also collect dust, and moisture from condensation dripping down windows. In no time a fresh coat of paint starts to look shabby.

Replacement sills can be made with 18mm. resin bonded plywood, set on battens and faced with laminate. Thereafter a quick wipe over will keep the sill looking as new.

See page 13 for details of working with laminate.

Remove the old sill and screw 2in. × 1in. battens to the brickwork.

Cut plywood or chipboard to size and screw it to the battens with countersunk screws. Drill starter holes for the screws. The back edge must be well sealed to prevent damp penetration. Use a mastic compound.

Cut the laminate to size and stick it down. Apply a slightly oversize lipping piece to the front edge and trim back before fixing the sill laminate. If excess condensation is likely, use a waterproof resin adhesive to stick laminate to the sill.

A NEW PANE OF GLASS

If you have never cut glass before or you do not own a glass cutter ask your supplier to do the cutting for you. Measure the frame first. The new pane of glass must be $\frac{1}{8}$in. smaller than the width and length of the frame. Check that the diagonals are equal in case the frame is out of square.

Your supplier will also advise on the type of putty you need (it varies with metal and wood window frames) and the type of glass. Different types are needed for, say, a greenhouse.

If you need a circular piece of glass, make a cardboard template of the shape for your supplier to cut to.

The glass in wood frames is held in place by special pins called sprigs. Glass in metal frames is held by special clips; the existing ones can be used again if you are careful not to damage them.

Wear a pair of old leather gloves to lever out the broken glass from the rebates, starting at the top. Difficult pieces will be released when the old putty is cut out with a sharp chisel.

Remove the old sprigs which held the glass in place. Clean off all remaining traces of putty. Paint the frame immediately with a priming paint. (a)

Press a strip of putty with your thumb and forefinger around the entire rebate. Dipping your hands in water, at intervals, will prevent the putty sticking to them. (b)

Press the new glass into place applying pressure only on the edges – never in the middle. (c)

Use the edge of the chisel to tap new $\frac{5}{8}$in. sprigs at 6in. intervals around the rebate. Then apply another strip of putty as before. Use a putty knife to angle the putty to match surrounding windows. (d)

Trim off surplus putty visible from the room side of the glass. Allow to harden for a week before painting. (e)

The Menace of Woodworm

Woodworm and dry rot are the main enemies of timber. Regular checks must be made on all the timber in and around the house – especially those out-of-sight areas in lofts and cellars where damage can spread unnoticed for months or years.

Several species of woodworm are likely to attack the house timbers. Eggs are laid in any small crevice or crack. Each egg hatches a larva which bores through the wood until it reaches a point just short of the surface. The larva has grown on its journey by feeding off the wood and it is now ready to enter the chrysalis stage where it remains before emerging at the surface as a beetle. As it emerges, fine dust is driven out, surrounding the tell-tale small hole in the wood surface.

So, when looking for woodworm, these are the signs you will be hoping *not* to see.

The beetle then continues the cycle. It mates and the female lays more eggs in crevices. It is because the beetles can fly that the damage can spring up in areas all over a loft or elsewhere.

It can take as long as three years for the larvae to reach the beetle stage though the beetle itself dies soon after laying its eggs.

Most people have heard of the furniture beetle since this is most common in furniture and structural timber. It is about $\frac{1}{8}$in. long. It is likely to attack softwood, plywood made with animal glue and furniture made of softwood or dry hardwood.

The spring and summer months are the best times to treat the trouble with insecticide since at this time of year, the beetle emerges to lay more eggs.

Death watch beetle attacks mainly old oak. It can be located by the ticking noise it makes. If it is allowed to remain in the wood it will eventually do so much damage that a structure can collapse.

A rarer species is the powder post beetle which attacks the sapwood of hardwoods. This can launch its attack in a timber yard and from there be carried to joineries in hardwoods which are then made into furniture or other things. The beetle emerges in May.

The house longhorn beetle is the most likely enemy to be found in the house roof. This is about $\frac{1}{2}$in. long. The hole it makes on emerging from the wood is oval in shape and a minimum of $\frac{1}{8}$in. wide. These are larger than the holes made by most other types of beetle.

Strangely, this type is most common in Surrey – being comparatively rare in other parts of the country. Under Building Regulations all structural timbers in certain parts of the country must be treated to prevent infestation. Any bad attack should be reported to the Princes Risborough Laboratory of the Building Research Establishment at Princes Risborough, Buckinghamshire.

Since the larvae lives in the wood for about four years, there are few flight holes to reveal its presence; so detection is difficult.

TREATMENT

Having identified the likely type of beetle attack, what can be done?

It is possible that, despite finding a number of holes, there may no longer be any larvae present in a structure. Provided the timber has not been weakened in the attack, no drastic steps need be taken. Just squirt some suitable insecticide into the holes in the surface, not forgetting cracks and joints – just in case.

Always buy a reputable brand of insecticide. There are spray-on, injection, or brush-on types available but remember, no insecticide can be applied to painted or varnished surfaces.

For minor attacks apply a generous brush coat of insecticide, taking special care with crevices or cracks. This will make sure that any larvae near the surface are killed – as well as any newly laid eggs.

Complete the treatment by making a few small holes and injecting insecticide into each one.

Wear gloves when handling insecticides and extinguish any naked lights – insecticides are flammable and give off fumes. So, if treating a loft or cellar, use a torch if an electricity supply is not provided.

Although, as was said earlier, summer is the best time for treatment since this is when the beetles emerge to lay eggs, if you see the tell-tale signs at any other time of the year then start treatment immediately. Repeat the treatment again in the spring and continue to do so for several years if a severe attack is discovered.

Should no new signs of attack be noticed at the end of a year then you can be fairly certain that the trouble has ceased.

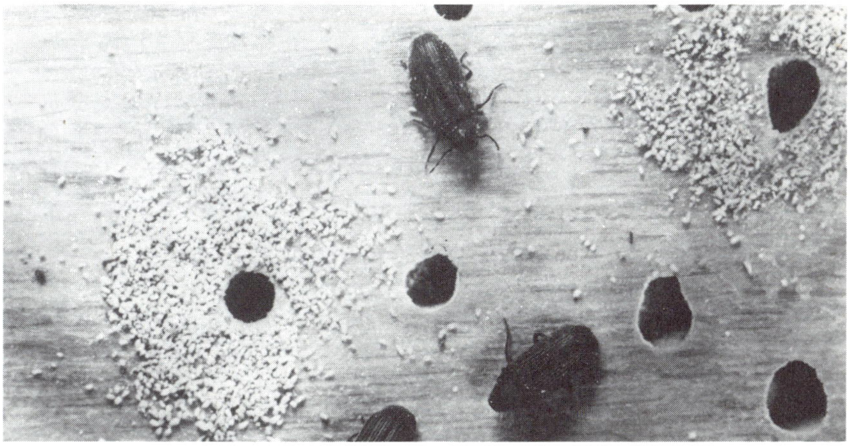

Dry and Wet Rot

Signs of wet rot round a kitchen window. Note the wrinkled and flaking paint.

Preventing rot is much better than curing it. Paint gives excellent protection – provided the coat remains unbroken and the timber is in a sound condition when the paint is applied.

Numerous preservatives are available. There are water soluble chemicals which are odourless and often colourless and can be painted over when dry. But rain will wash them away if they are not painted.

Solvent types are quicker drying and so can be painted over more quickly. They are not affected by rain.

Creosote is a cheaper type of preservative; it resists rain, is non-corrosive for nails and so is ideal for applying to garden fences. However, the fumes it gives off will damage plants near it so be careful when using it.

Dry rot is far more serious than beetle attacks and must be treated immediately it is discovered, since it spreads rapidly.

It is, in fact, a moisture carrying fungus which raises the moisture content of timber. The fungus consists of microscopic spores produced from mature fruiting bodies developed on decaying timber.

The spores are carried in the air and thus may be distributed over a wide area. Should they fall on timber with a moisture content higher than 20% they germinate, and mycellium (a cotton wool-like substance) develops fruiting bodies which liberate more spores into the air. And so the cycle continues.

The mycelium can penetrate crevices in masonry to reach timber. The timber, in time, will become brittle and cracked and will become a darker colour.

The main attacking fungus is *Merulis lacrymans*. Its white strands grow and form yellow and grey patches. The fruiting bodies form later and produce rust coloured spores.

Another fungus is 'cellar' fungus. This has black strands. The correct name for this type is *Coniophora cerebella*. The popular name arises from the fact that it is found in wet conditions – typical of cellars – or where a roof has been leaking.

There are other types of fungi which are classed as wet rot because they do not spread from the immediate area of damp. Decay with these is most active where timber has been damp for a while and where there is poor ventilation.

Dry rot is usually hidden from view – under ground floor timber, in roof rafters, or in eaves that have been boxed in. These are the places to look.

A musty smell often indicates trouble, so take up a few floorboards – especially near skirtings – and use your nose. Stick a knife into the wood in a few places – if it goes in easily there could be trouble.

Examine anywhere where there are water pipes – especially areas like under closed-in baths.

Check that airbricks are not obstructed and that the damp proof course has not been covered with piles of earth or similar material.

Provided the rot is in a comparatively minor stage, you can treat it yourself. Cut out all affected timber and burn it immediately. Since the cause of the rot will still be present make sure it cannot start up again by providing permanent ventilation. The rot can infiltrate brickwork and concrete so sterilise any of these adjoining the trouble spot with heat from a blowlamp.

Fix new timber to replace any cut out. Coat the new timber immediately with preservative, or buy pressure treated timber in which preservative sinks right into the wood during the process, which is not possible to achieve simply with a brush coating. Your timber yard should be able to supply you with pressure treated timber, though it will cost a bit more and may have to be specially ordered.

If a brush coating is used, then be generous with the preservative. Apply it when the timber is dry. Coat any parts exposed after cutting, and be especially careful to give a good coating to any areas in contact with brickwork.

Very serious attacks of rot should be handled professionally. The British Wood Preserving Association, 62 Oxford Street, London, W1N 9WD, will give you a list of firms who will guarantee their work for twenty years.

Tiles for Walls and Floors

Although ceramic tiles provide a hardwearing and long lasting floor-covering or wallcovering, accidents do happen and the odd one may get cracked.

Individual tiles can be replaced without disturbing the surrounding areas, or old tiles that have become crazed can be replaced with decorative tiles or tile-prints (see page 74).

Lift out any loose undamaged tiles, scrape off the old adhesive and refix with ceramic tile adhesive. Check before fixing that the new tile will lie flush with the surface. If it projects, chip away the old backing material (probably a sand and cement mix) from the wall or floor.

The grout line between wall tiles inevitably becomes discoloured. Rake out the old grout and refill the joints with new material. New grout cement is bought in powder form and mixed with water to a thick, creamy consistency.

Wall tiles can be given a colour change by painting with gloss paint.

If necessary, use a chisel and hammer to chip the old mortar or adhesive from the wall before re-fixing a loose tile.

If the new tile is likely to be splashed by water use a waterproof adhesive.

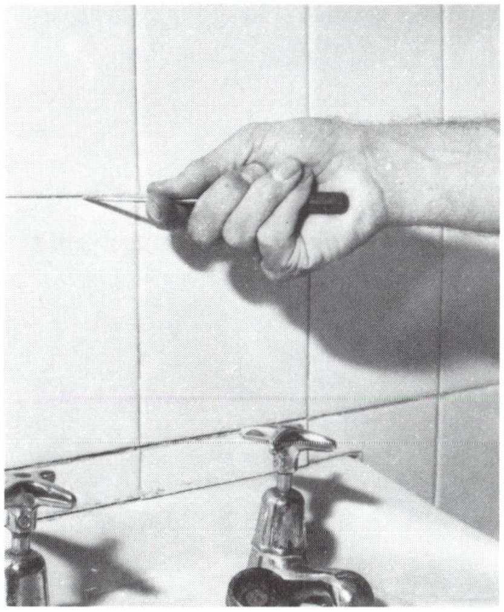

An old, worn screwdriver is ideal for raking out discoloured grout.

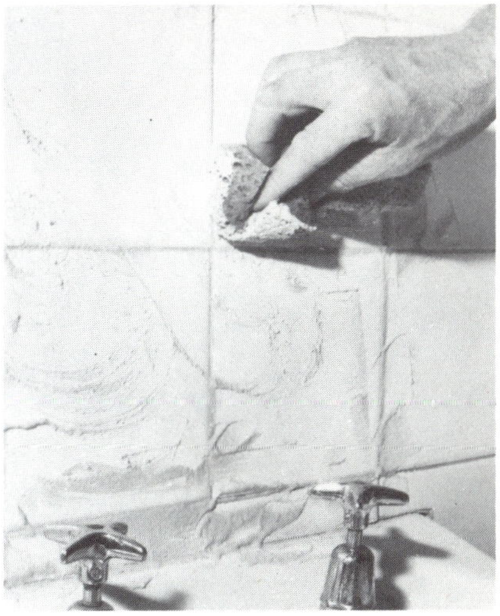

Use a damp sponge to spread the new grout cement over a square yard of the tiles at a time. Do not mix more grout than can be used in half an hour or it will set in the mixing container. Do not mix fresh grout on top of any that has started to set – the fresh material will also start to set immediately.

Before changing the colour of tiles with gloss paint, rub down the surface with coarse emery paper to provide a key for the paint. Defective grout between tiles must be replaced before painting.

If ceramic floor tiles are not laid on an even bed of adhesive, they will be cracked by chair legs, or other pressure exerted on hollow spots. Remove a damaged tile (see page 69) and replace using correct adhesive. Alternatively, fix as for quarry tiles (page 72).

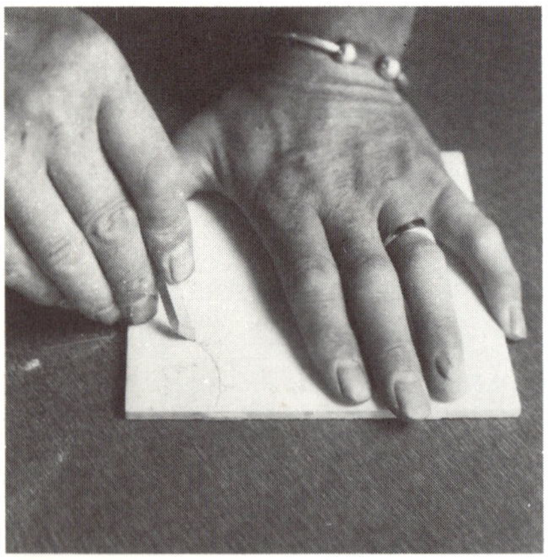

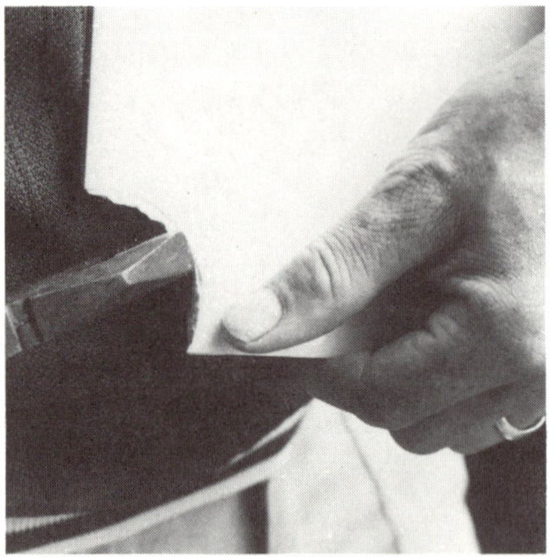

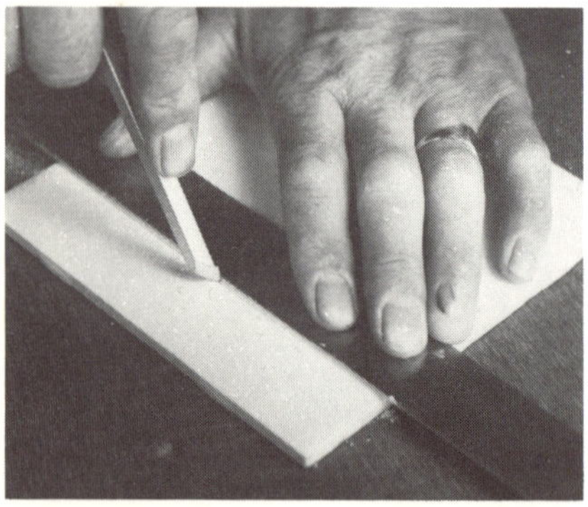

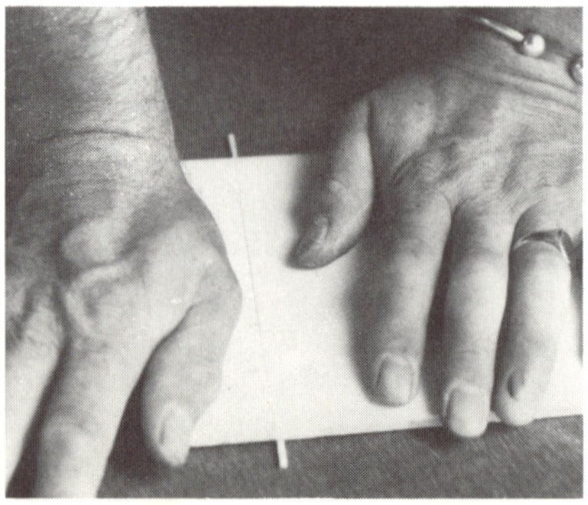

VINYL TILES

It is always worth while buying a few extra tiles at the outset in case any have to be replaced at a later date. It is sometimes difficult to find individual tiles of a particular design or colour if they are a few years old.

Never simply re-lay floor tiles that have lifted. The lifting indicates that the original adhesive was the wrong type or that the floor is damp. Any damp must be remedied before a new tile is laid, otherwise the problem will re-occur.

Originally, the tiles may have been laid on felt paper or hardboard. If it was felt paper then this will inevitably be torn off when the damaged tile is removed; if so it must be replaced. The new tile, though the same make, may be a slightly different colour. This could be because a protective coat of sealer was applied to the original tiles. Sealer is available from d-i-y shops. To obtain a uniform colour, may necessitate sanding off the old sealer from the entire floor before re-coating.

Cut shaped tiles by first scoring deeply along the intended cut line with a ceramic tile cutter.

Nibble away the waste area with pincers.

Make straight cuts by scoring the tile with the cutter held against a straight-edge.

Lay the second tile over two matchsticks and press down firmly to break the tile along the scored line. Narrow strips of less than about $\frac{3}{8}$in. have to be nibbled away with pincers as for shaped tiles.

A partly lifted vinyl tile can be pulled off, taking care not to disturb surrounding tiles.

Remove remaining fragments with a scraper or a broad, worn chisel, working from the centre outwards.

Spread adhesive on the floor. Warm the tile in an oven to make it pliable. It can then be arched and lowered into position.

To mark out a border tile, a spare tile of the same dimensions is needed. (A) Lay the replacement tile (B) over the last full tile in the row. Position the spare tile with its edge against the skirting and draw a pencil line where its other edge meets the replacement tile.
Cut along the pencil line and fit the replacement tile.

Cutting around obstacles involves a difficult marking-out procedure. A simpler method is to make a cardboard pattern of the required shape and transfer this to the replacement tile. A 'Mimic' tool can be employed for tracing awkward shapes.

Use a sharp knife (such as a Stanley type) to cut slits along the back edge of the tile so that it can be slotted into position. The slits will not be noticed behind the obstacle.

Make a cardboard pattern for L-shapes at corners.

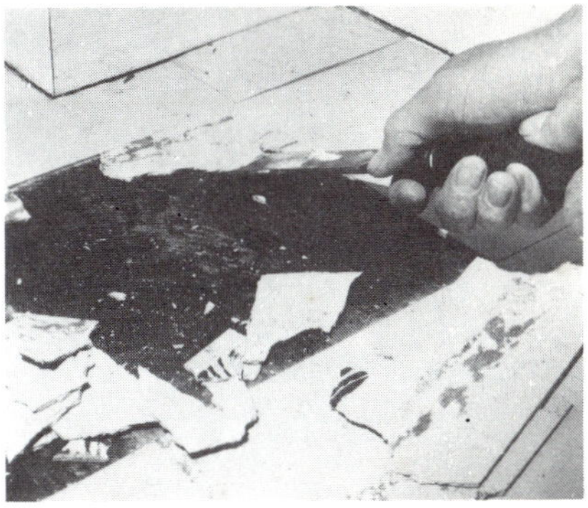

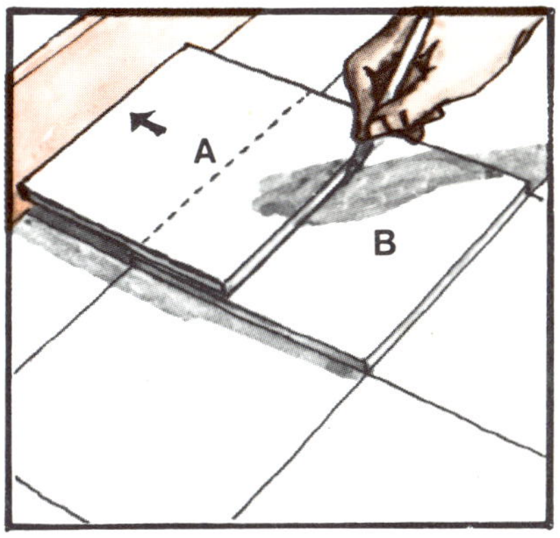

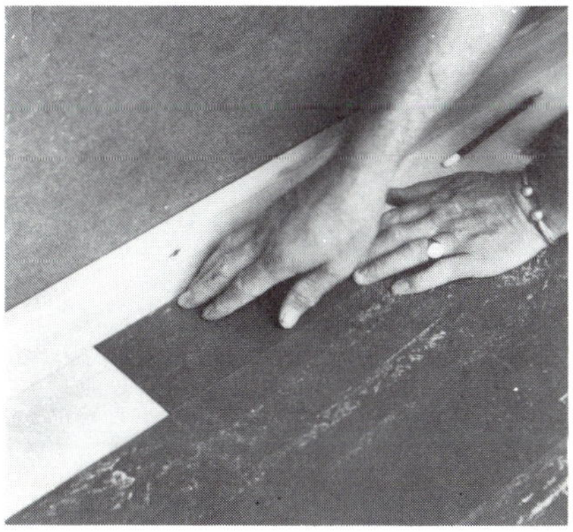

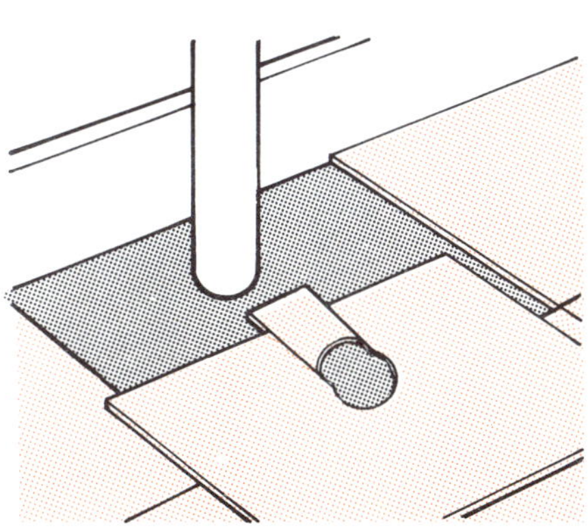

QUARRY TILES
These are difficult to cut. Awkward shapes are best cut into several smaller, convenient shapes and laid jigsaw-fashion around obstacles.

Replacement tiles and adhesive are available from builders' merchants.

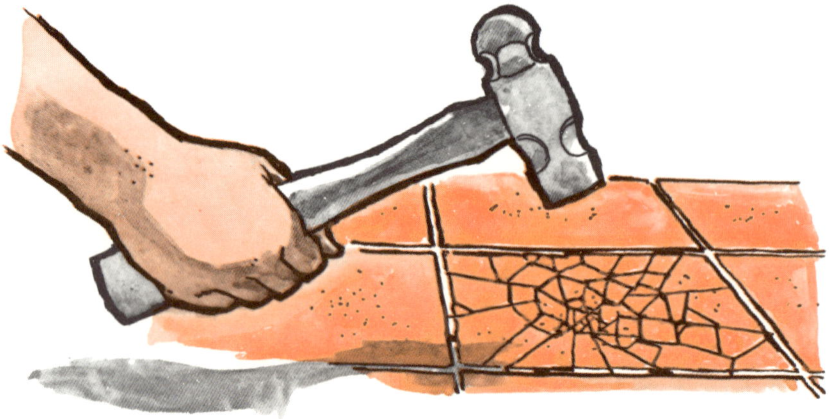

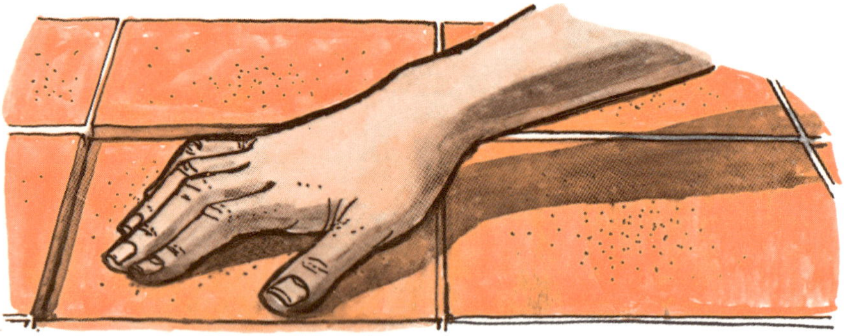

Craze the complete surface of the damaged tile. Then, using a cold chisel and a hammer, remove the tile, working from the centre outwards.

Check that the new tile lies just below the surface of the surrounding tiles. If it does not, then chisel away the old mortar (probably a sand and cement mix) from the floor.

Spread a mix of one part cement to 3 parts sand on the floor and press the new tile into place. Remove surplus material which squelches to the surface.

After 24 hours, fill the joints with a mix of 1 part cement to 4 parts sand. Use a trowel to force it well into the joints.

Your supplier may agree to cut a tile for you for a small charge. This is worth paying since the tiles can crack easily if cut incorrectly. If you have to do it yourself, mark the cut line on the back of the tile. Place the tile on the edge of a brick and tap along with a cold chisel and club hammer.

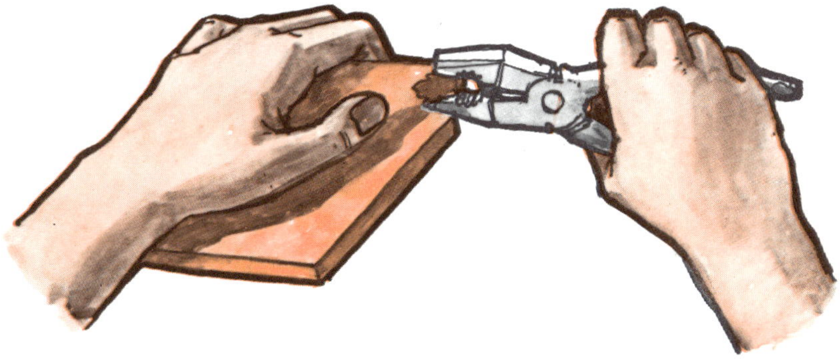

Tap the tile against the edge of the brick to break it along the line. Awkward shapes must be nibbled off with pliers or pincers as for ceramic tiles.

fireplaces

Fumes and heat from an open fire can cause tiles to become crazed or the pointing between the bricks to deteriorate.

Make sure you can obtain a matching tile before removing a damaged one. This can be a problem with older fireplaces.

A possible alternative to replacement is to cover the defective tile with a Sellotape tile print. These are available in a variety of designs and pictures, but do not use them where tiles get excessively hot near the fire opening. Alternatively fit a non-matching decorative tile.

Where damage is extensive, the whole fireplace can be covered with new, thin decorative ceramic tiles.

A crazed ceramic tile can be covered with a suitable decorative tile print. These are just pressed into place after peeling away the paper backing.

a

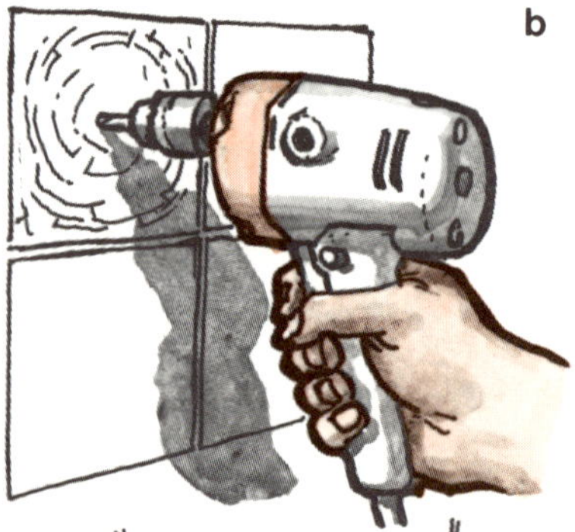

b

Where crazing is extensive, to give a new look, fix modern ceramic tiles over the existing ones, using the special adhesive supplied with the tiles. (a)

To remove a single, damaged tile, first drill through the centre with a masonry bit fitted to a brace or power drill. (b)

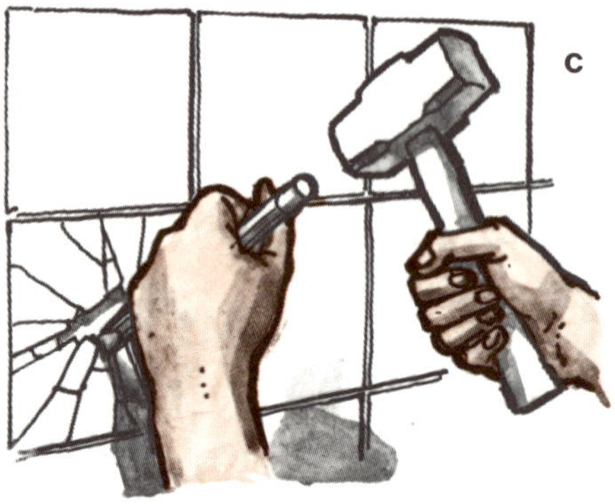

c

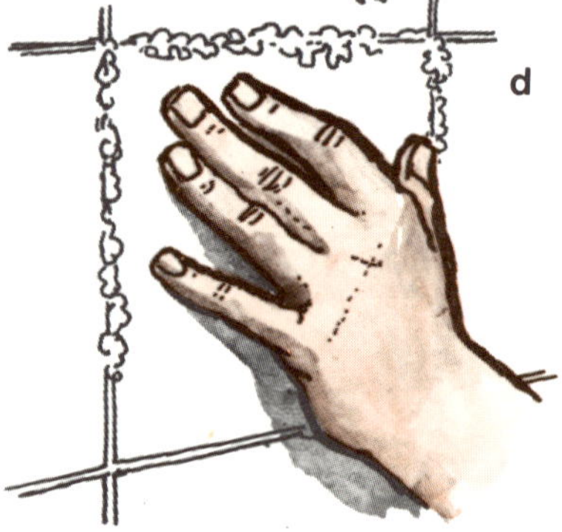

d

Use a cold chisel and club hammer to chip away the tile from the centre outwards. Be careful not to damage surrounding tiles. (c)

Replace the new tile using ceramic tile adhesive. Use a thick enough layer to leave the tile flush with the surface of the others. (d)

e

Use a damp cloth to remove any adhesive that squelches to the surface. Special grouting cement is available to fill in the joints. Press this well into the joints using a damp sponge. (e)

BRICK FIREPLACES

If a brick fireplace needs repointing, the mortar used depends on whether the fireplace is used for an open fire or whether it is purely decorative. If still in use, make a mix of 1 part Portland cement, 3 parts lime and ten parts heat resistant sand (called silver sand).

If purely decorative, then you can use the normal brickwork mortar mix (see caption below).

It is possible to add a coloured dye, available from builders' merchants, to the mortar mix to give a more decorative effect. In this case, though, you would have to repoint all the joints between the bricks in order to achieve a uniform overall effect.

Replacing a brick Usually it is the hearth surround that suffers the most wear and tear. Consequently loose bricks are usually found here. Corners are especially prone to damage.

a

Remove the loose or damaged brick using a bolster chisel and club hammer. Chip through the mortar joints to form a clean, square-cut cavity. (a)

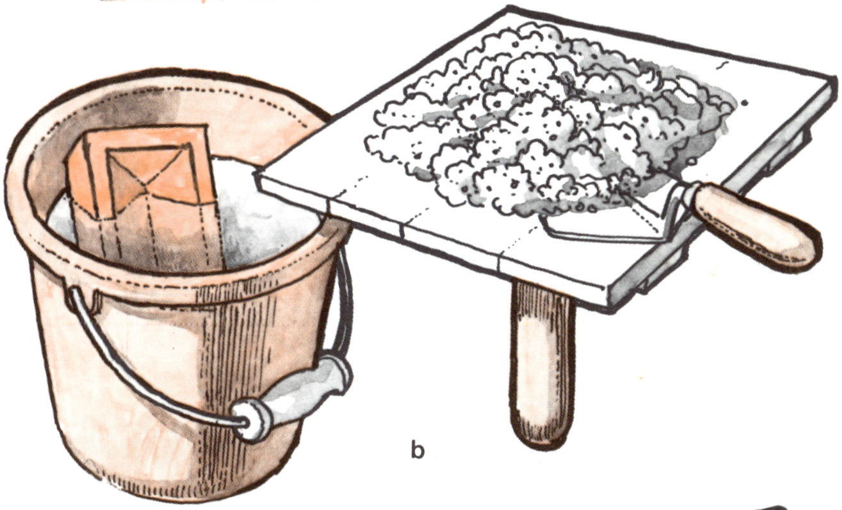
b

Wet the brick with clean water before applying a mortar mix (3 parts sand to 1 part cement) to the bricks with a trowel. (b)

c

Use the handle of a trowel to tap the brick into place. Any of the cement that squelches to the surface should be cleaned back to leave a ¼in. recess in the joints. When the cement has set the joint can be repointed. (c)

STONE FIREPLACES

The replacement of loose or broken stones is covered in the illustrations and captions on this page.

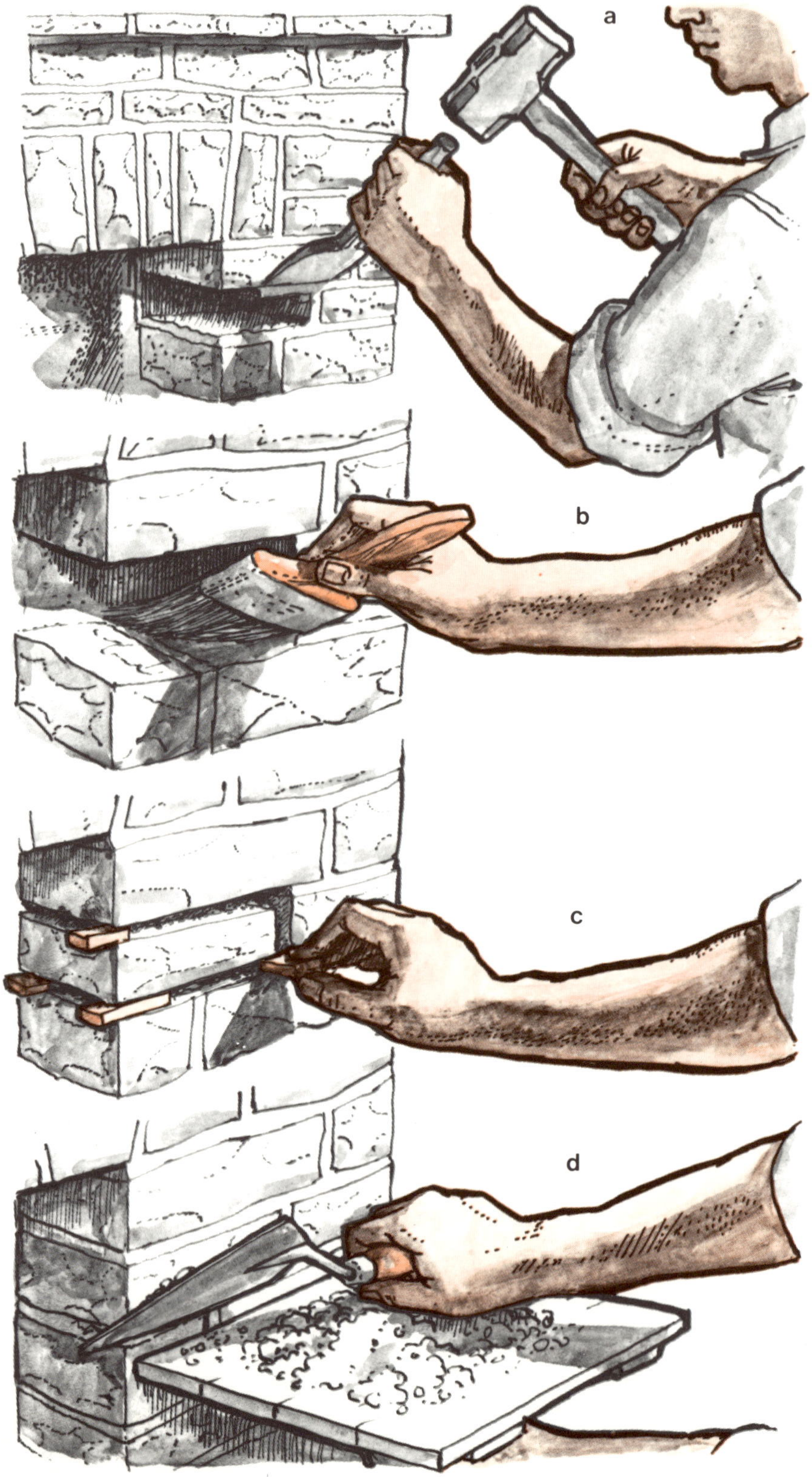

Remove the loose stone by chipping away the existing cement mortar. Clean out the cavity. (a)

Wet the stone with clean water and butter on a mortar mix (as for bricks). (b)

Replace the stone, using wood wedges to hold it in line with the existing stones. (c)

When the cement has set, remove the battens and re-point. (d)

MARBLE FIREPLACES

It is possible to replace a broken piece of marble with an epoxy resin adhesive.

If very small fragments of the broken piece are lost, the gaps can be filled with the adhesive. Follow adhesive manufacturer's instructions closely. Usually the cavity from which the piece came and the back of the broken piece have to be dusted down with a stiff brush and rubbed with fine glasspaper to make a key for the adhesive.

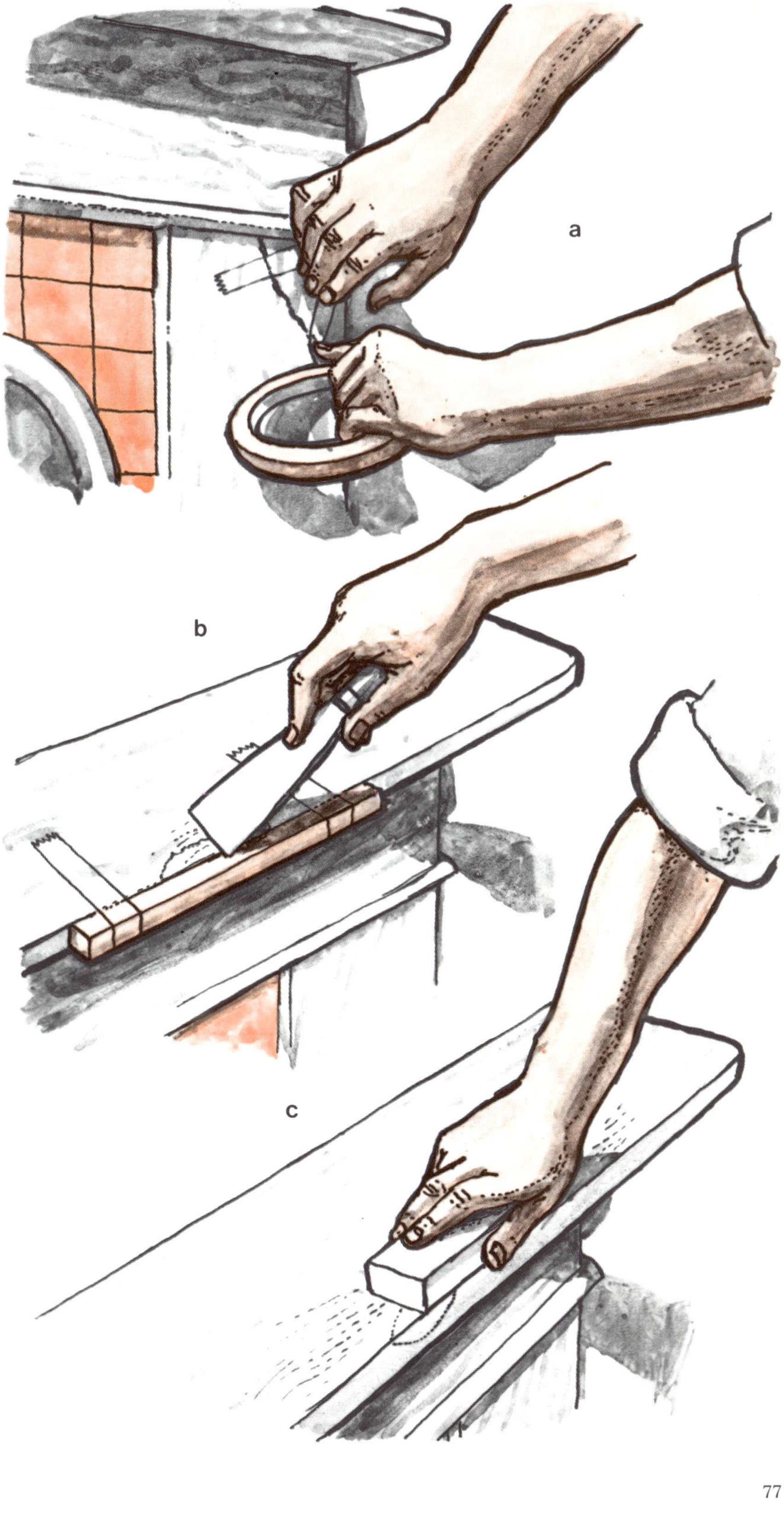

Apply the adhesive to both surfaces and then press the broken piece back into place. Hold it in position until it has set, using adhesive tape. (a)

Fill in chips with epoxy resin adhesive. If necessary, add a vegetable dye (available from builder's merchants) to match up with the colour of the marble. (b)

When set, wash the repair, using clean water to remove all traces of adhesive. Finally, polish the area with a fine carborundum stone. (c)

FIREBACKS

A fireback protects the chimney structural brickwork from being damaged by heat and smoke. Provided a fireback is only slightly cracked, repairs can be made with plastic fireclay.

The cracks must be raked out thoroughly to remove all dust particles. Use a trowel and wire brush. Soak the cracks thoroughly with water. Work the fireclay well into the cracks and remove excess clay before it dries.

Where damage is more extensive a new fireback has to be fitted. The old fireback can be chipped away with a club hammer and cold chisel.

A new fireback often has to be fitted in two sections. They are normally supplied as a complete unit so ask your supplier to separate the lower and top sections for you.

When the two sections are fitted in the fireplace, the joint between them should be filled with fire cement using a trowel. The throat of the chimney may then have to be built up using a sand and cement mortar.

Minor cracks can be repaired with plastic fireclay. The crack is cleaned out thoroughly, dampened with water, and the fireclay forced into the cavity and smoothed level. (a)

Extensive damage will mean fitting a new fireback. First, remove the broken back section, using a club hammer and brick bolster. When the upper and lower sections have been taken out, remove the loose infill that forms the backing. (b)

Fit the lower half of the new fireback accurately in position. Fill the recess behind the lower half using a mix of 1 part cement, 1 part lime and 10 parts sand. (c)

Fit the top section in place and fill the cavity behind it in the same way. (d)

Use a rendering mix of 1 part cement to 4 parts sand to angle the top of the fireback to meet the chimney brickwork and form the 'throat' to the flue. (e)

d

e

Looking After Gates

If a gate will not close properly or is sagging, try tightening the hinge screws. If they will not tighten, remove the hinge, fill the screw holes with wooden plugs and replace screws.

Alternatively, use thicker screws, enlarging the holes in the hinges with a drill and countersink bit.

If the hinges themselves are faulty, fit new ones.

WOODEN GATES

Examine the joints in a wooden gate to see if they are loose or have come apart. If they have, then take the gate off its hinges, prise all the joints apart and clean out all the old paint and glue. Apply preservative to all areas. Reassemble the gate using waterproof glue in the joints. Before the glue sets, check that the gate is square.

To reposition a sagging gate post, you must first dig it out. Inspect the base for rot. Cut back to sound timber if necessary. Apply a liberal coat of preservative.

Fix the post vertically in position and fill the hole round it with rubble and concrete. If necessary, insert a concrete spur to stand the post on.

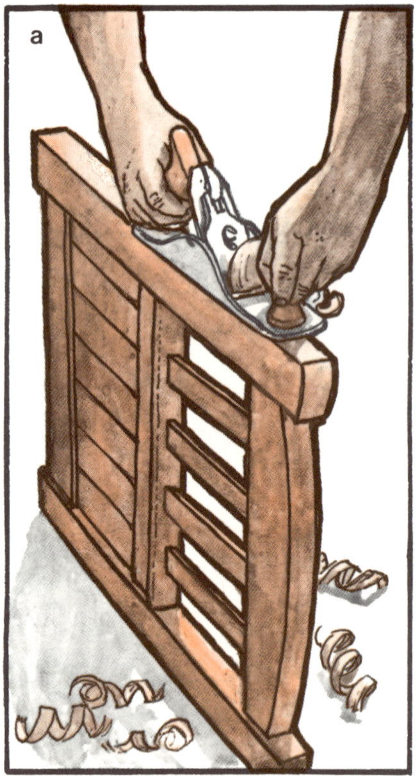

If the gate jams and the problem is minor, try planing off a small amount from the upper part of the stile to a bevel before repainting. (a)

Poor joints can be reinforced with galvanised metal brackets available from d-i-y shops. (b)

If a new gate post has to be fitted, dig a hole at least 18in. deep. Refix the post and pack out the hole with rubble topped by 6in. of concrete (mix as for fence posts). (c)

A damaged panelled garage door can best be prepared by screwing an exterior quality plywood panel over the entire lower section and into the outer framework of the door. It is important to see that the back of the panel is primed before fixing and that all edges of the panel are primed thoroughly before painting. (d)

IRON GATES

Rust is the biggest enemy of iron gates. Make regular checks to ensure that the paint film is unbroken. Even small cracks are an open invitation to rust.

Iron gates often have cracks where moisture becomes trapped and sets up corrosion.

Deal with any rust spots immediately, by scraping the corrosion back to bright metal (it need not gleam). Tackle minor spots with emery paper, or use a wire brush followed by abrasive paper.

It must be remembered that paint alone is not a complete protection against rust; a metal primer is needed underneath.

Before priming, clean the surface with white spirit. Apply the priming coat at once or rusting will start again immediately.

A blowlamp and scraper is a useful and speedy method for cleaning rust from an iron gate.

Brush primer well into any rivets, bolts, nails or screwheads. Give all metal edges a second coat (after the first has dried) as they are susceptible to knocks.

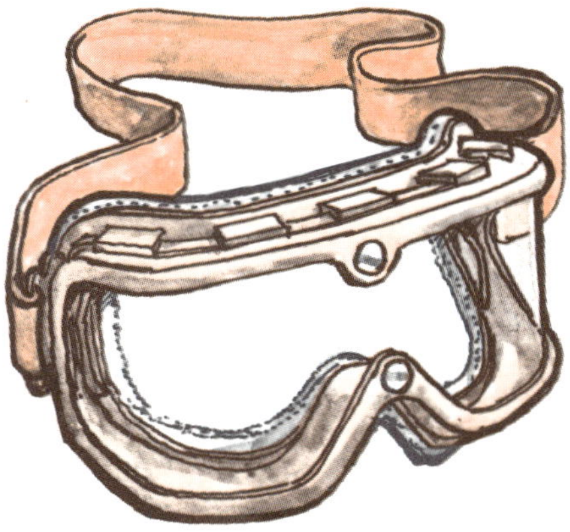

If using a wire brush to clear away rust, it is advisable to protect the eyes from flying particles by wearing goggles.

Looking After Fences

One popular type of fence is a close-board type consisting of feather-edged pales (vertical boards) fixed to horizontal arris rails. The arris rails are slotted into sockets in the posts and the pales overlap each other. The height of this type of fence can be anything you like.

Interwoven and interlocking panels are cheaper than the close board fences. Here the wide ready-made panels are simply fixed to the posts with nails. The interwoven type does have gaps in the woven sections but still provides a reasonable amount of privacy.

Interlocking panels ensure complete privacy.

Palisade fencing is a traditional boundary fence. It is ideal as a backing for flower beds since it allows plenty of sunlight and fresh air through. The pales, again, are fixed to the arris rails, which, in turn, are secured to the posts.

Ranch-style fences are becoming more and more popular as simple boundary fences, especially between front gardens of neighbouring houses. Consisting simply of a couple of horizontal timbers fixed to evenly spaced posts (often only about 2 or 3ft. high), their attraction is ease of maintenance as well as their appearance.

Rustic fences consist of a series of criss-crossed rustic poles and give a garden a rural atmosphere.

Trellis is usually used as a capping section along a solid fence. It is lightweight and cheap and is especially useful for supporting climbing plants.

Ranch-style plastic fences in various heights have several advantages over wooden types. They will not rot and are virtually maintenance-free. Normally a quick wipe over with a damp sponge will keep them shining white.

INSTALLING A FENCE

Unless special care is taken to install a new fence, you can be sure that it will not be long before you have to do some maintenance work on it.

The first thing to do is to mark out, with a string line, the path that the fence has to follow.

Place a wooden peg into the ground at either end of the boundary and then tie a piece of string between them, pulling it tight.

The holes for the posts now can be dug. The spacings will vary according to the type and height of the fence. Manufacturers of individual fences will give you guidance – though in some cases, such as 6ft. long panel types, the posts will obviously be set 6ft. apart.

The most difficult part of installing a fence is digging the holes for the posts. The easiest way out is to hire a post hole borer from a local hire shop. These are turned into the ground rather like a corkscrew. After each few turns, the borer is withdrawn and the earth collected on the blades is deposited nearby. This is continued until the hole is the right depth.

And this depth is another point on which you will need individual advice from manufacturers. However, as a general rule, if the fence is under 5ft. high, then a 2ft. deep hole is required. Above 5ft. the hole should be 2ft. 6in. at least.

The kind and size of posts is often decided for you since many fences are supplied in kit form. However, if you select a type which leaves you the choice then you can opt for one of two things:

For appearance sake, most people prefer to use all-timber posts. However, these will rot in the ground eventually (though with preservative treatment this risk can be considerably reduced). The alternative is to buy concrete spurs from a builders' merchant and use these in the ground with the timber posts bolted to them 1ft. or so clear of the soil.

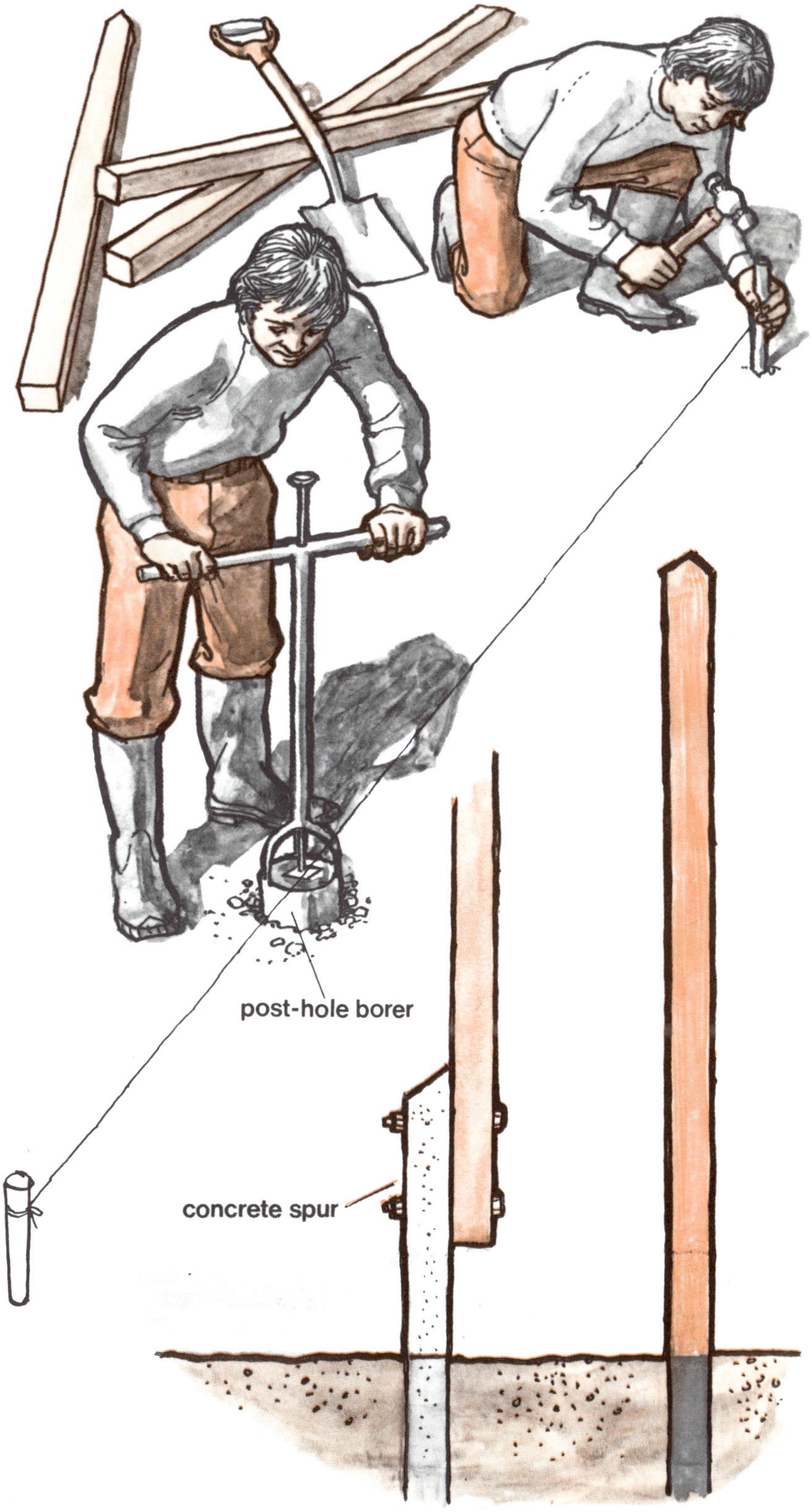

The thickness of posts varies with the fence type. Normally, for fences up to 5ft. high, 4in. square posts are needed. Above this height 5in. × 4in. posts are needed. If possible, choose Western red cedar as the timber for posts; this is particularly durable.

Earlier, mention was made of preservative treatment. The best way to protect the bottom of a post from rotting in the ground is to soak it overnight, before fixing, by standing it in a bucket of preservative. Creosote is a common preservative, though there are several other proprietary types available. This method will allow the preservative really to soak into the timber – something that does not happen with a straightforward brush application. Since fumes from creosote will damage plant life, a non-bituminous preservative is preferable in certain situations. Solignum is one example.

Fixing the posts A post can be fixed in the ground in one of several ways. It is not sufficient to insert a post in the ground and ram earth around it. After only a short while the soil would become softened by rain and the post would lean one way or the other.

Even a complete filling of the hole round the post with concrete has its disadvantages. The timber, in time, will shrink away from the concrete leaving gaps for rainwater to run into and eventually cause rot. And, of course, should you ever want to remove the fence to install a new type, removing the posts will be a real problem.

Soak the bottom of the posts overnight in preservative.

Check that the post is upright with a spirit level.

The best method is to pack out the bottom of the hole with pieces of brick, rubble and other hardcore. This will allow good drainage. Put in the post and the hole can then be filled with alternate layers of earth and rubble, finishing with a layer of concrete.

Check that the post is upright with a spirit level – it must be truly vertical.

You can, of course, choose concrete posts. They will not rot but they do have the disadvantage of being unattractive to look at.

If you do want to use them, you can, for economy, make concrete posts yourself using a simple timber mould. The method of casting these is to make a wooden frame of two sides (to the correct post length and thickness) and with end pieces attached. Nail this framework together and also nail several small timber battens across the top opening.

A concrete mix of 1 part Portland cement: $1\frac{1}{2}$ parts sand and 3 parts of coarse aggregate is needed. To reinforce each post, a mild steel rod can be used down the centre.

If holes are needed through the posts for fixing wire fencing to them, insert oiled steel pins through the concrete when wet. These can be withdrawn after the concrete has set.

If wood fencing panels are to be joined to the posts, then wallplugs set into the posts during casting will allow wood fillets to be screwed to them to support the fence panels.

A simple timber mould for making a concrete post.

Constructing the rest of the fence
If the fence is a type supported by arris rails, then these should be located in the sockets of the posts as the posts are fixed in the ground.

Erect all the posts and rails before fixing the fencing itself. If pales are being used, then the first one must be fixed absolutely vertically or the whole lot will be out of line.

This is also important with close board fencing and palisade fencing.

At the bottom of the fence, a gravel board is needed to help prevent rot setting up in the bottom edges of the fencing. A gravel board is simply a horizontal board secured to the fence posts.

Although fixing methods vary with panel fences, in general the posts will be set with 6ft. gaps between them for 6ft. panels and the panels nailed to the posts. Always use galvanized or aluminium alloy nails which will not rust.

The tops of the posts should be shaped to allow rainwater to drain away. So cut them to a bevel shape. Obviously it is much easier to do this before a post is fixed.

An alternative method is to cap the posts with a piece of zinc or aluminium, nailed in place.

If the fence was not pre-treated with preservative, then see to this as soon as the fence is up. More information on preservatives is given on page 84.

The top of a fence post can rot through rainwater collecting on it. Cut the top of the post at an angle to allow water to drain away. Remember that it is easier to do this before setting the post into the ground.

Alternatively, cap the post with zinc or lead. Use these methods on an old post that is rotting from the top. Cut back to sound timber first, though.

FENCE MAINTENANCE

Garden fences have to withstand a regular buffeting from the elements. If they are not fixed firmly, the wind can blow them down; if they are not protected with preservative, they will inevitably rot.

A regular inspection of fences is essential. If damage is spotted early on, it can usually be dealt with effectively and cheaply by making a simple repair. The longer it is left, the worse it will become and eventually replacement may be the only course – at a price.

The simplest form of maintenance is to apply wood preservative or creosote to a fence. This will protect it from rot, woodboring insects and fungus.

Check manufacturer's instructions to find out how often the treatment should be repeated. Usually it must be repeated every other year.

Unlike other preservatives, creosote will darken the colour of the wood. Choose a creosote which has a British Standard number on the container and apply it when the timber is dry – creosote will not penetrate damp timber.

DAMAGED OR ROTTEN FENCE POSTS

If a fence post has rotted at the bottom and the damage does not extend too far up, cut out the rotted section and refix the post to a concrete spur available from a builders' merchant.

If damage is extensive, the whole post will have to be dug out. This can often be hard work. Buy a replacement post of the same size – usually they are 4in. square or 5in. × 4in.

Before attempting to remove the post, take off one fence board from either side of the post and remove also the gravel boards on either side. You may have to cut through the arris rails in order to free these from the post.

Wedge the fence temporarily in position on either side of the post.

Dig out the earth around a post that needs renewing. If the post cannot be removed easily, it will be necessary to rig up a lever using an old post, bricks, ropes and nails. The fulcrum can also be on the side of the post nearest the man. In this case he would push down on it.

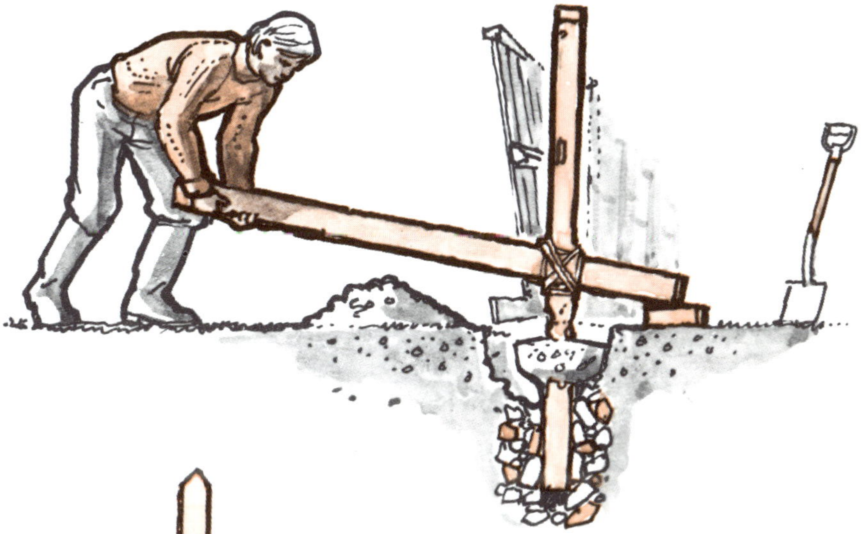

Fit the new post in a hole at least 2ft. deep. Fill it with rubble, well rammed down for the first 6in., then pack at least 1ft. of concrete (dryish) mix before covering the top with soil. The mix should be 1 part cement to 4 parts all-in aggregate. Check with a spirit level that the post is upright both at the front and side.
Refix the arris rails, fence boards and gravel boards.

CONCRETE SPURS FOR PARTLY ROTTED POSTS

Buy a concrete spur with pre-drilled fixing holes and get the right length of bolts for fixing the fence to the post. The length needed depends on the width of the spur and the fence post.

As before, free the post from the ground and wedge the fence in position while work is being carried out.

Dig out the old post stump. Place the concrete spur in the hole; this must be at least 2ft. deep. Check with a spirit level that the spur is upright. Pack out the hole with bricks and rubble to keep the spur in position. (a)

Fill the top of the hole with concrete (using the same mix as for fence posts).
Before the concrete has set, fix the post in place and tighten the bolts firmly. Finally refix the fence. (b)

FEATHER EDGED BOARDS

Where boards have not been treated with preservative they are likely to warp and split.

Isolated boards can be removed and new lengths be inserted without removing the whole section of fence between two posts.

If a board is in reasonable condition and has just worked loose, there is no need to buy a new length.

Use aluminium alloy nails for re-fixing.

Remove the damaged board by punching the fixing nails through into the arris rail. Use a nail punch and hammer. If the nails can be extracted with a claw hammer or pincers use one of these. Often the nails will have rusted making extraction impossible. (a)

Repeat this operation by punching the nails securing the thick, outer edge of the adjacent board through into the arris rail. (b)

Fit the new board by sliding its thin edge under the thick edge of the adjacent board. Board edges usually overlap by about $\frac{1}{2}$in. Nail through the overlapping edges into the arris rail. (c)

A broken end can be re-secured by making a frame of 1in. square battens around the recess in the post. Screw the battens to the post. See that they are well treated with a wood preservative before fixing – especially the end grain. (a)

Proprietary extension brackets are simple to fit if the end of a rail breaks. (b)

Repair brackets are made also for splits which occur in the middle of a rail. (c)

If buying a completely new rail, it should be at least 3in. longer than the space between the posts. The extra amount allows for the tenons which go inside the posts. (d)

If a fence post is loose, it can be pushed out of position temporarily to enable both ends of the new rail to be slotted into the recesses. If posts are solid in the ground, fit one of the rail ends into the recess; fit the other end using one of the methods already described. (e)

ARRIS RAILS

The arris rails which stretch between the posts are slotted into recesses in the post ends. The ends of the rails are shaped where they enter the post. Often this shaped end breaks off when the rest of the rail is in good condition. Here, a simple repair can be made to avoid having to buy a new rail.

If a complete rail needs renewing, it is best to shape the ends of the rails into tenons so that they can slot into the posts as before, provided the posts are loosened first.

GRAVEL BOARDS

At the base of a fence there is often a wide piece of timber – about 6in. × 1in. – which is called the gravel board. This prevents damp rising up and damaging the fence boards.

The gravel board must be kept clear of a build up of soil and plants.

If the board gets damaged or shows signs of rotting, replace it immediately. It may be slotted into a recess in the fence posts or be nailed to wood blocks.

Having removed the old gravel board, dig a small trench. This makes it easier to manoeuvre the new board into position.

Fix a 2in. × 2in. batten to each fence post. Screw them in place keeping their tops in line with the bottom of the boards. These battens are then ready to receive the gravel boards.

Nail the gravel board to the wood battens. It should be flush with the front of the fence. When the positioning is correct, fill in the trench.

Where concrete posts are encountered, drive pegs into the ground alongside the posts. At least 1ft. of each peg must be buried. Fix the gravel boards to the pegs.

Simple Furniture Repairs

It is surprising how often an uneven chair leg, a burn mark or a crack is allowed to remain for a long time to spoil the appearance of an otherwise attractive piece of furniture.

Many basic repairs are well within the scope of the ordinary handyman.

Even when a solid piece of furniture is looking really shabby, it need not necessarily be thrown on the scrap heap. It can be given a facelift to modernise it and keep it in service. Decorative coverings such as laminate, mirror tiles and veneers are not difficult to apply.

UNEVEN LEGS

If a chair has one leg longer than the other three, it is a simple matter to measure the even legs and saw a little off the long leg. After sawing, clean up the cut edges with fine glasspaper.

Where one leg is shorter than the others there is a choice. Either the three longer legs can be sawn down to match the length of the odd one or the odd

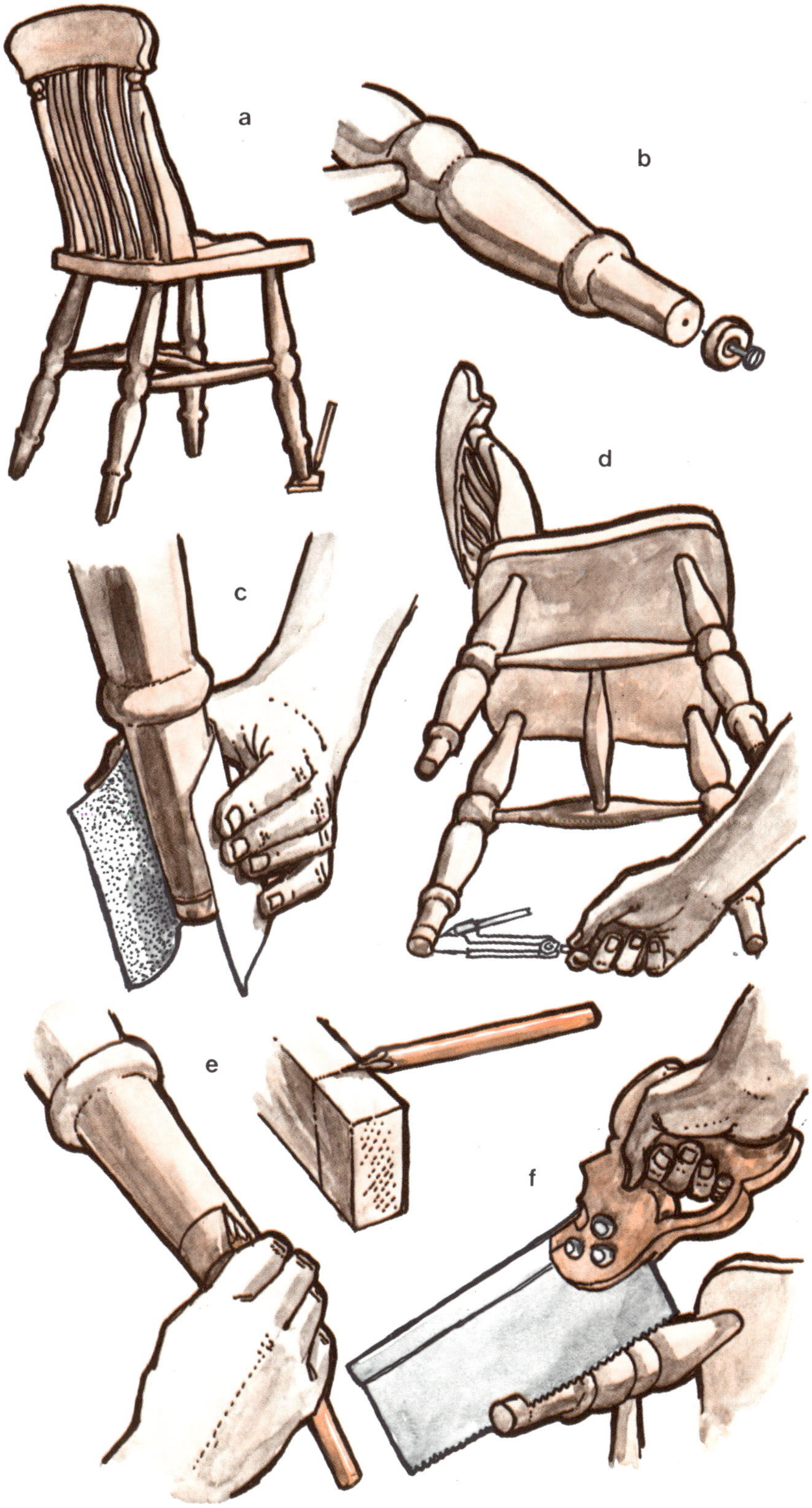

With the chair standing on a level surface, slip different-size pieces of wood under the shorter leg until the chair no longer wobbles. (a)

Trim the piece of wood to suit the shape of the leg, and screw it in place with a countersunk screw. Drill pilot holes for the screw in both the chair leg and the wood block to prevent the screw causing splits as it sinks in. (b)

Fill the joint between the new piece and the leg with wood filler. Allow it to set before rubbing it smooth with the grain and painting. (c)

Alternatively, use compasses to transfer the thickness of the block to the other three legs. (d)

Draw a guide line for the saw around all four faces of each leg. (e)

Saw down to the guide lines. Smooth edges with fine glasspaper. (f)

one can be built up with a wood block to match the others.

The latter will be less noticeable where a piece of furniture is to be painted, for there will be no problem about matching the wood block to suit the grain and colour of the leg.

A SPLIT LEG

Misuse of furniture on castors can cause the legs to split. Castors are usually screwed into a housing which, in turn, is located in a hole drilled in the underside of the leg. The housing is held in place by spikes that bite into the wood. After unscrewing the castor the housing can be prised out with a screwdriver.

SCRATCHES

Hairline scratches can often be made less noticeable by rubbing shoe polish of the same shade into the surface.

Deeper scratches that have penetrated through the protective coating on the wood can be smoothed out with burnishing cream.

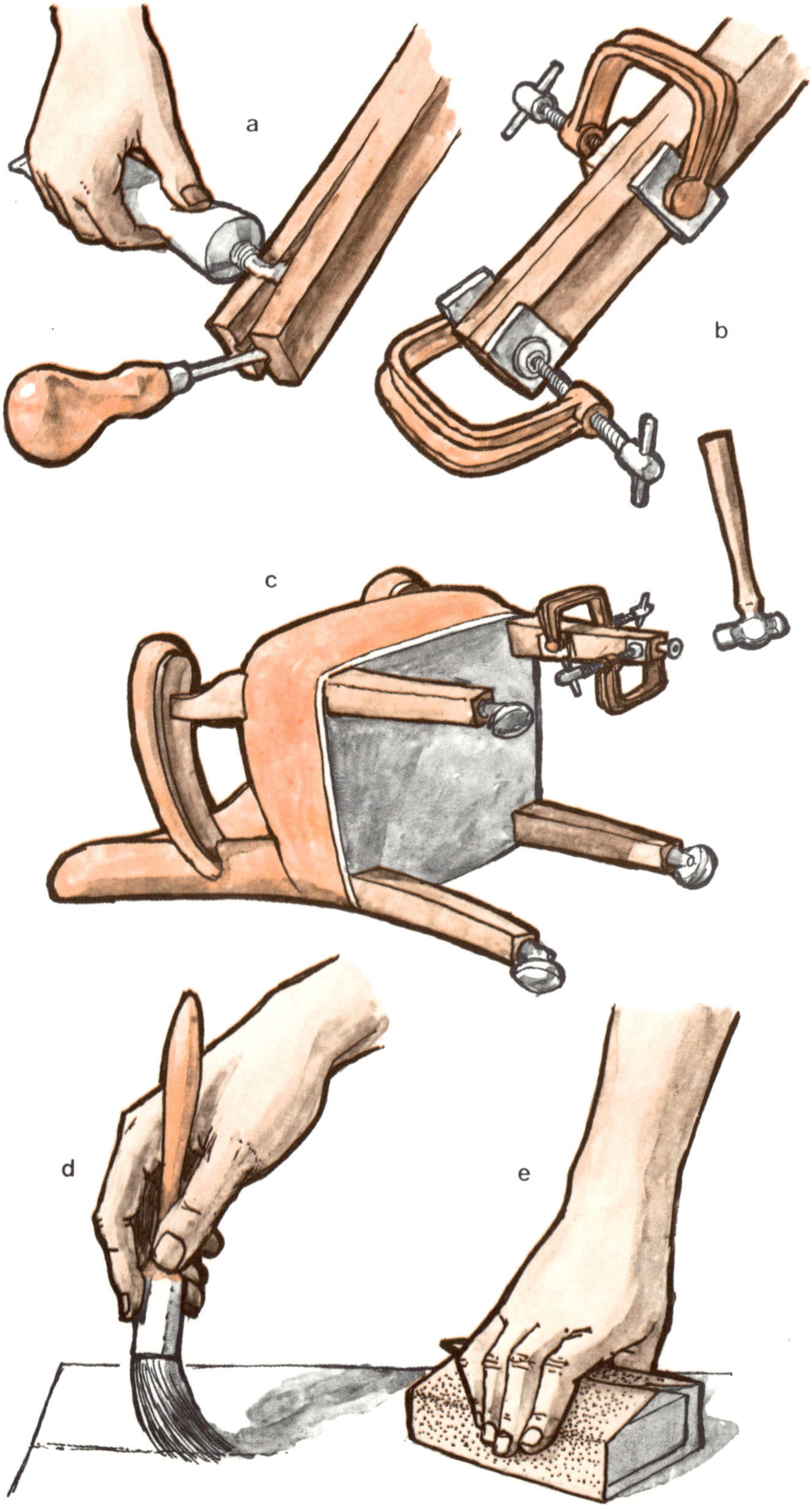

Wedge the crack apart so that woodworking adhesive can be squirted inside. (a)

Use G cramps to hold the legs in position while the glue sets. Clean off glue that squelches to the surface. (b)

Remove the cramps, knock back the spiked housing, screw on the castor. (c)

Fill deeper scratches with shellac varnish stain of the correct colour. This should be thinned with methylated spirit according to the manufacturer's instructions. Apply several coats with a small brush until the varnish is just proud of the surface. Then rub down the dry varnish with fine wet or dry abrasive paper. Finally use metal polish to bring the shine back to the surface. (d)

Rub down minor scratches with fine wet or dry abrasive paper until the scratch is removed. (e)

HEAT AND WATER MARKS

Furniture tops with a shellac or cellulose finish are liable to be stained by heat or water marks. Provided the mark has not penetrated through the protective coating to the wood, it can be removed with a mild abrasive such as burnishing cream.

HANDI-VENEER

Handi-veneer is a simple way of giving a new timber grained surface to an old piece of furniture. This has adhesive already on the back. It is fixed in position using a warm iron.

Use a sharp knife to scrape away the scorch mark completely. Rub the area with fine glasspaper.

Where the surface was previously covered with a clear finishing liquid (varnish, polish, etc.) apply transparent French polish according to the manufacturer's instructions. Several applications will be needed. Use fine glasspaper to rub down the area carefully. Finally, apply metal polish to bring back the shine.

Use burnishing cream to remove heat and water marks. Use a soft cloth and work in the direction of the grain. Fill cracks with plastic woodfiller. Allow to set and then glasspaper lightly until flush with the surface.

Apply a varnish stain which matches the colour of the wood. Finish with a clear finish where one was previously used.

Cut Handi-veneer to size with scissors; peel off the protective paper backing. (a)

Smooth it into place with heat from a warm electric iron. (b)

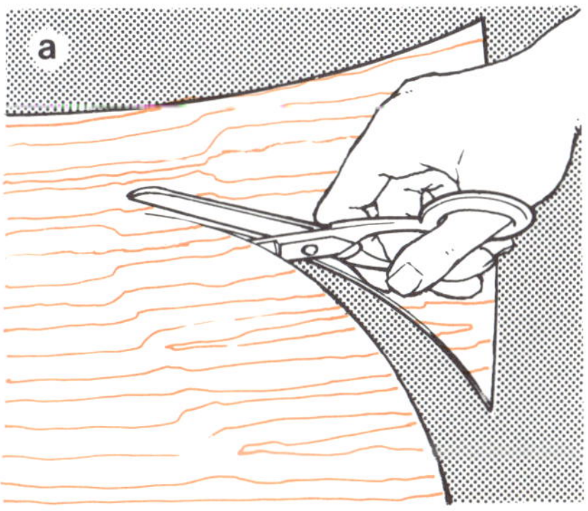

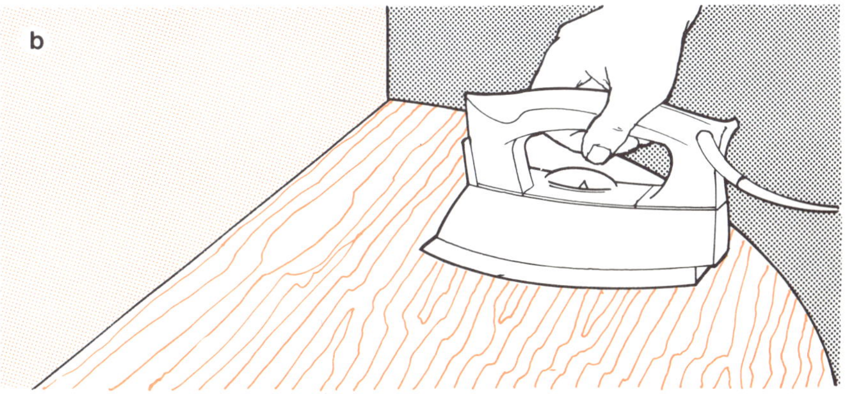

Adhesives for Everyday Use

Choosing the right glue to stick two things together can be a somewhat confusing business nowadays. Yet, if you know exactly what you are looking for, the extensive selection available will be very much in your favour.

Not so long ago there was very little choice and therefore repairs, whilst not exactly carried out on a hit or miss basis were not always successful.

If you use the right type of modern glue and the two items do not adhere, or soon fall apart, then the explanation will probably be that you did not follow the directions properly.

For example, you will always find that the directions say that the surfaces of the materials being joined should be clean, dry and free from grease and dust. This is not something that can be done by a quick wipe with a rag or by blowing dust from the surface.

It means clean them with soap and water, white spirit or whatever is appropriate for the materials in question.

You will find, too, that some glues will stick only to roughened surfaces, and others will work only on smooth, non-absorbent ones.

Do not take lightly warnings about using naked lights nearby or about providing adequate ventilation. Many glues have flammable bases and others give off vapours which can be harmful if inhaled for a long time.

ANIMAL GLUES

These glues are made from the skin and bones of animals and will stick leather, paper and wood. Two types are available, a cold setting type and a Scotch glue.

The latter has to be heated for use. When it cools it sets, and in a cold atmosphere, it can cool too quickly – before you have time to use it, for it starts setting immediately it is taken away from the heat. When using it to glue joints, it is essential to apply cramps for a longer period than with other types of adhesive.

One other disadvantage of Scotch glue is that it is not waterproof, but it is extremely valuable for work such as sticking down wood veneers.

Cold-setting animal glues are made in liquid form and take longer to set than Scotch glue. More time is available, therefore, to position the pieces being joined.

PVA

This type of adhesive is often specified for use in the manufacturers' instructions in a whole variety of products that come in kit form.

The name in full, is polyvinylacetate. The adhesive comes ready to use on wood, paper, fabrics, card and leather.

In woodwork, the adhesive (a white liquid) is applied to one half of the joint only before cramps are applied.

SYNTHETIC RESIN ADHESIVE

This is usually supplied in powder form for mixing with water.

Used for woodwork, these adhesives are resistant to water, acid and heat and will not stain the wood. The glue is stronger than the wood it sticks together so that once it has set, a joint cannot be dismantled or pulled apart without damaging the wood.

How long the glue takes to set depends on the temperature in the workshop or room. The hotter it is, the shorter is the setting time. The type of hardener used can also vary the setting time. Check this point before buying.

Cramps must be applied to hold the parts in place whilst the adhesive sets. When all the joints have been glued, the pieces can be cramped together.

EPOXY RESIN

An expensive adhesive which is supplied in two parts, which are mixed together. One part is resin, the other is hardener.

There are many brands available. Although it sticks virtually anything to anything, is really unnecessary in many cases where an effective cheaper substitute will do.

The big advantage with epoxy resin adhesive is that non-porous materials – rigid plastics, glass and metal can be joined together effectively.

It will resist such things as boiling water, acids and heat.

It is usually supplied in two tubes – resin and a hardener. Usually these have to be mixed in equal proportions. Heat, applied gently, will reduce the setting time.

CONTACT ADHESIVES

These really do stick on contact. Made of synthetic rubber and resin glue, they must be applied to both surfaces being joined. When they become touch dry the two surfaces are brought together and a strong bond is formed immediately.

Obviously, since the positions of the two parts being joined cannot be adjusted after sticking, their positioning must be absolutely right first time. Nowadays you can get non-drip contact adhesives, which are to be recommended as they are easier to work with and do allow some time for adjustment. Contact adhesives are suitable for joining together plastic laminate and wood, rubber, leather, fabrics, cork, etc.

GENERAL PURPOSE ADHESIVES

It is always worth while keeping a tube of one of the vast army of general purpose glues in the house. They stick together a whole variety of materials – paper, leather, fabrics, pvc, plastics, china, glass and so on. Two things they will not stick are expanded polystyrene and polythene. The latter can only be joined by heat welding, so never waste time attempting to do the job with an adhesive.

Resurfacing a Path with Cold-laid Macadam

One of the speediest methods of improving the appearance of a path or a drive is to use a cold-laid macadam, such as Colascrete.

An alternative method is to use Colas, a black, treacly liquid in conjunction with coloured stone chippings.

An average size garden path should take no more than one good mornings' work to re-surface, using either of these materials.

Colascrete is sometimes used by itself and sometimes it is spread over a layer of Colas. The sub-floor is the deciding factor.

If economy is important (assuming that either system is acceptable to you) which of the two systems is adopted depends on the dimensions of the area to be treated. Colas on its own is certainly more economical for larger areas.

Both these treatments can be used on a variety of surfaces – ash, gravel, concrete, clinker, and so on. The basic techniques are the same for both materials.

USING COLAS

Taking the Colas and stone chippings system first, the first decision to be made is the quantities of materials to order. This is related directly to the conditions of the surface to be treated.

Should you be dealing with an old, concrete sub-floor, then the Colas can be spread out much further than on a loose surface.

As a guide you can use one gallon of Colas to cover about 5 square yards on concrete. For loose surfaces, one gallon can be used to cover only $1\frac{1}{3}$ square yards.

These figures are based on minimum and maximum spreading. You will have to use your own judgement as to how much to use on reasonably firm surfaces that fall somewhere between concrete and loose ash.

Some time before the work is going to be tackled, you should start to prepare the site so that it will be ready in time.

Preparation really means getting rid of any grass, weeds, or moss.

This must be done thoroughly, or some months after the macadam is laid, the more persistent weeds could grow up through the new surface.

Use a proprietary weedkiller – any gardening shop should stock a selection of brands – and allow it plenty of time to do its job. Tar-oil winter wash will get rid of moss. Follow manufacturer's directions closely.

Another thing to bear in mind is that the ground should be shaped to allow for drainage. In other words the centre should be higher than the sides, or there should be a slight tilt where this is practicable. Nothing is worse than a new drive that is dotted with puddles during rainy spells.

Immediately prior to using the macadam, sweep away any loose material such as leaves, from the surface.

If there are drains or manhole covers in the work area, then cover these to make sure they do not become clogged or blocked with the new material. They can be masked with pieces of plywood, weighted down at the edges with bricks and stones.

Next the Colas must be transferred from the container – a drum – to a one gallon watering can.

Then, in order to make sure that the correct quantity is spread over the area evenly, three things should be done.

First, the site can be marked out roughly into small plots of equal size according to the distribution coverage decided upon – for example, one gallon to three square yards.

Second, as it is not easy to control the flow of liquid pouring from the spout of the watering can, an old dessert spoon tied securely to the spout of the can so that the liquid will gush out on to its concave side will give much more even distribution.

It must be an old spoon as it will not be usable for its normal purposes afterwards!

If two people can work together, then so much the better. Whilst one is brushing out the Colas with a yard broom to leave an even surface film, the other one can be distributing the stone chippings. In any case the chippings should be laid within twenty minutes of spreading the Colas. In this period, the liquid will remain tacky enough for the chippings to adhere to it.

The chippings can be scattered with a shovel though a few extra handfuls will probably be needed here and there to cover any bare or thinly covered patches.

In general, 50kg. (about 1 cubic foot) of chippings will cover an area of about 7sq. yds.

The newly laid chippings must be compacted immediately by rolling. It is advisable to keep a bucket of water handy so the roller can be kept wet at all times because, if the roller is used dry, it will continually be picking up a coating of tacky stones.

A thorough rolling will knit nearly all the stones and Colas together. Any odd, loose stones can be swept away later using a light broom. Extra rolling at this stage, though not essential, will add to the performance and appearance of the surface.

USING COLASCRETE

On many drives, there is a place which, because of its location, is subject to much more wear than any other. The places to note are the entrance itself, any sharp bends where car brakes will be regularly applied, or under trees where the surface remains damp for long periods.

Should there be any deep depressions or even potholes in the surface, Colascrete will be needed to fill them. This is a much more solid material and comes in bags. Use a shovel to transfer it from the bag to the hole and spread it out level with a rake. Compact it thoroughly with a garden roller.

To lay Colascrete, follow the same preparation techniques as for Colas some time before the day that the new surface is to be laid.

All weeds and plants must be

Fill potholes with Colascrete.

Rake level and compact with roller.

Spray on Colas from an old watering can and brush out with an old yard broom.

removed, the surface shaped to facilitate drainage, manhole covers and drains masked and the area swept clean.

Colas liquid, as was said earlier, often has to be used prior to spreading the Colascrete. Whether or not you have to use it depends on the surface being covered.

If the existing surface is of loose material – or concrete – then it must be used. Otherwise you can omit it.

Over concrete, use one gallon to eight square yards. On other surfaces use one gallon to five square yards.

Brush out the liquid, working in one direction only. Allow about twenty minutes for it to set.

At the end of the drying period, the liquid will have changed in colour from brown to black.

Use a knife to slit open the polythene bags containing the Colascrete. Empty the contents on to the ground. Try to shake the material over a square yard or so – not in a heap. This makes spreading it out to the required thickness an easier task.

Use a rake to spread the material to a thickness of about $\frac{3}{4}$in. over a convenient section. As far as possible, avoiding standing on the fresh material as you are spreading it as it will stick to your shoes.

As soon as each section is raked, it can be compacted by rolling. As before, keep the roller wet to avoid it picking up.

Doubtlessly, you will leave depressions at first through over-rolling some areas. Should this happen, add more material to make up the depressions to surface level before re-rolling. Continue in this way until the whole area is complete.

A few days later, the area should be given another roll. At this stage, you may choose to scatter some decorative chippings which will break up the overall colour of the drive.

Colours of Colascrete are red, green, or black.

The decorative chippings come in small polythene bags from your Colascrete supplier. Just scatter these in handsful over the surface prior to the final rolling, which will bed them in.

As a guide to the quantity of Colascrete needed – you will require about 2cwt. to cover 40 sq. ft. to a thickness of about $\frac{1}{2}$in. when rolled.

Emptying Colascrete from bag. (a)

Raking level. (b)

Compacting with a roller. (c)

Scattering decorative chippings before final roll. (d)

The Use of Ladders and Scaffolds

Any home maintenance job is easier if it can be done in comfort. This means that all the necessary tools should be easily to hand and the work area should be within easy reach.

There are few difficulties in arranging this when a job can be done with your feet planted firmly on the ground but problems do arise once you have to scale the heights.

Few people enjoy working at a height. It is never particularly easy to concentrate fully on what you are doing while half your thinking is devoted to keeping your balance.

This applies even if you are standing on a small step stool. Many people are aware of the alarming statistics concerning injuries in the home from falls, sometimes of only a few inches. The rate is high and it could happen to you if you do not put safety first.

So let us look at the various means available which enable us to work in comfort.

LADDERS

If you own a ladder then you must ensure that it is kept in good condition. A wooden ladder, provided it is made of well-seasoned wood and is stored, horizontally, under cover, will give a lifetime's service.

Irrespective of how it is stored, inside or outside, a coat of exterior grade varnish will prevent it from rotting.

Never paint a ladder – it will not be possible to see if rot develops. Through clear varnish, the condition of the wood is always evident.

Before use, no matter how good the ladder looks, examine it carefully for damage.

If you buy or hire a ladder, you have to decide which is the best type for your particular needs.

This depends on several factors. First, the correct height. Work out the highest point at which you are likely to stand on the ladder and buy a ladder that will extend 3ft. 6in. above this point. You might also take into account that, should you move house, you might need a bit more height in the future.

Ladders come in one, two or three sections. The three section ladders are easiest to store since they fold down to a smaller length.

Their disadvantage is that they are awkward to erect unless you get the knack by using them constantly.

You might be better off going for a two-section one, but the best way to find out is to go to the nearest large stockist where you can try your hand with different types.

Ladders are generally of wood or aluminium. The latter are much lighter and need no maintenance.

Should you buy an aluminium ladder wipe it all over before use. There will often be a coating of grease on it and this could mark paintwork.

Always erect a ladder on a firm base. Should the erection site be on earth, or other soft ground provide a platform of

Erecting a ladder.

boards to prevent the legs from sinking in.

To stop the legs slipping backwards a batten can be screwed to the board as a stop ledge.

On firm ground get someone to stand at the foot of the ladder – not on it – so that they can steady the ladder.

If help is not available, tie the bottom rung to any firm, permanent support – a downpipe, for example – or use a weight such as a sandbag.

Correct footwear is conducive to easier and more comfortable working from a ladder. Plimsoles are not suitable – the rungs will soon make your feet ache. Always wear shoes, not boots; the latter are clumsy and locating the rungs is not easy when wearing them.

Make sure that your shoes are not muddy as your feet could easily slip off the rungs.

When erecting a tall ladder for work on a roof or gutter, it is useful for the beginner if a helper is on hand.

Get the helper to hold one end of the ladder firm whilst you raise the other end.

Position it, vertically against the house wall. Now pull out the base so that the correct angle can be achieved. The distance between the house wall and the base of the ladder should be one quarter of the ladder's height.

Make sure that at least three rungs of the ladder extend above the level of the gutter or whatever height you are working at.

Tie the ladder to a ring bolt screwed to the fascia and this will prevent it from sliding sideways.

Never lean a ladder against a plastic guttering as it is not strong enough to withstand this sort of weight.

There are various proprietary aids and gadgets which make working from a ladder much easier. Standing on the rungs for long periods is uncomfortable, whether or not the correct footwear is worn, but you can use a ladder platform. The 'arms' of this device lock on to the rungs, leaving a small step for you to stand on.

As an alternative, ladder cripples (brackets) can be fixed to two ladders to support a scaffold board thus providing a continuous working surface.

Painting the underside of an overhanging roof would mean reaching backwards if a ladder stay were not used. And reaching backwards in this way is only advisable for a circus trapeze artiste, not a handyman.

A ladder stay locks on to the top rungs of the ladder and the other end rests against the house wall, so that the ladder is held firmly a couple of feet away from the wall.

You will certainly need an S-hook to hold your paint can or a container for the tools needed for the job you are doing.

Never lean out sideways to reach a work area. Only work in areas that are within comfortable reach.

When you have to move the ladder to a new work position, never slide it along with the top resting against the wall. This could damage pebble-dashing or paintwork. Lift the ladder clear of the wall before repositioning.

To make sure that the ladder never has a chance of rubbing or damaging fresh work, start painting on the right hand side of a window or wall if you are right handed. Left handed people should work from left to right.

Where you have to work above a window opening and the ladder has nothing to rest against, tie a stout batten to the ladder parallel to the top rungs. The batten should be wider than the window so that it rests against the walls at either side of the window frame.

SCAFFOLDS

No matter how safely secured a ladder is, there are many people who start feeling jittery as their feet leave the bottom rung.

In the past, these people had little alternative but to call in professional help for high-up work. Not only has this become very expensive, but it is also frustrating for the man who enjoys maintaining his home and knows that an unreliable professional might well skimp awkward pieces of work.

A stout batten tied to the ladder helps when decorating over a window.

For this group of people there are scaffolding kits available, generally known as tower platforms. Several manufacturers produce their own type.

Before you start thinking in terms of tubular bars joined together in a complicated arrangement with nuts, bolts and anchor plates – the sort of thing that can be seen on a construction site – let me reassure you that the home handyman tower platforms are much more simple.

Indeed if they were as complicated and time consuming to assemble and dismantle, I would not recommend them to the amateur.

To whet your appetite, let me tell you at the outset that even if you have never used one of them before, then it will take you no more than ten minutes to erect a 16ft. high scaffolding that is completely safe to use. And if you had another pair of hands to help you, that time could be cut in half comfortably.

The great advantage of these kits is that all your high-level jobs can be carried out in ground level conditions. This mean that you will feel secure and can concentrate all your thoughts on your work.

Furthermore you will not get tired so quickly as when working from a ladder. There is no need to be continually going up and down and repositioning the ladder for new work areas.

As I have said earlier, there are several types of these kits made. Basically, however, they are all similar. I use a Junior Kwiktower kit which is fairly representative of all other models.

The tower is comprised of a series of tubular steel frames which interlock and are built up gradually to whatever height is required.

Each frame consists of two vertical uprights joined by two horizontal bars. At the top of each upright is a spigot (a bottle neck). At the other end is the full diameter of the tube socket.

A straightforward tower.

To join up the frames, all one has to do is to locate the sockets of successive frames on to the spigots of the frame below.

Thus the first frame is placed at ground level with the spigots pointing upwards. The sockets of the next frame slide over the spigots of the previous one and are pushed down firmly to anchor it.

That is all there is to it. No tricky fixings in sight. Frames, incidentally, are either 2ft. or 4ft. wide.

Before running through the exact assembly technique, it is worth listing all the various accessories. Some are essential to a basic tower; others bring out the full versatility of the towers.

The basic essential is a horizontal brace. This is a long tubular bar with rings on both ends. The rings are of a slightly larger diameter than the frame members.

The brace is used to prevent the tower 'doing the splits'. It is secured diagonally to the first two frames set at ground level. The rings simply slide over the tubular uprights.

When the required height of a tower has been reached, an enclosed working platform has to be assembled. To achieve this, there are handrails and guard rails which are similar to the brace and are fixed in the same way.

The working platform itself is comprised of thick boards which butt up to each other. On the underside are wood strips which lock up against the tubes to keep the platform in place.

Depending on how and where a platform is to be used, there is a choice of five different bases or feet. Where a tower is being used on level ground, socket bases are fixed to the base frames.

If a platform is being arranged that will run continuously alongside a wall giving a long, low level platform, then trestle feet are fitted.

Such is the width of the frames that, in many cases, whereas two of the feet may be resting on a flat concrete path running alongside the house, the other feet may be on uneven ground. For this and all similar situations, such as where one or more feet are resting on steps, there are adjustable bases. These can be altered to take up any unevenness in the ground.

Mobility is the key factor of these tower platforms. To enable them to be repositioned conveniently for a new work area, there are castors.

Finally, there are rubber feet, should you want to convert some of the frames into a workbench.

Now for the assembly method in more detail. First of all the correct bases – trestle, adjustable, castors or whatever, have to be selected for the ground conditions.

Let us take a typical example and discuss a situation where two of the legs are on firm ground and two are on uneven ground. As we have just seen, adjustable legs are needed.

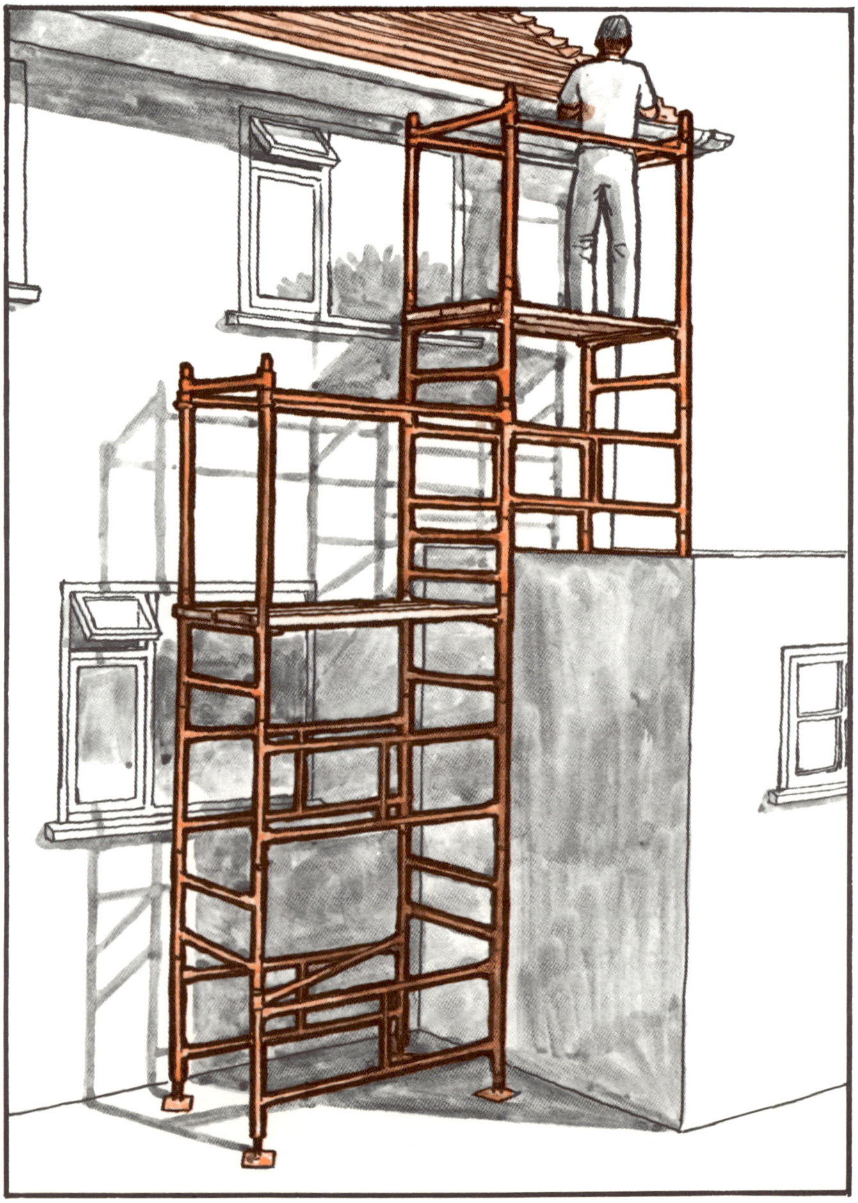

Cantilevering over a roof.

These are placed on their approximate positions on the ground. The first two frames are located on the feet (spigots uppermost). The horizontal brace is now slotted diagonally to join up these two base frames.

The next two frames are added at right angles to the base frames. It is at this point that any adjustments to the bases have to be made.

One of the most important things about a tower is that it must be built up perfectly level. So a spirit level is needed to check it.

Provided, these base frames are level, the frames placed above them will automatically be level.

By laying the spirit level on the horizontal crossbars of the second frames just placed in position, and adjusting the bases as necessary, a true level can be found quickly. From there on more frames are added until

Decorating a stairwell.

the required working height is reached.

A safe foothold can be provided, during construction, by laying a couple of the working platform boards in position whilst you slot on more frames.

At this point a word of warning about ascending tower platforms. At no time should you attempt to climb up the outside of a tower as it could topple over. You must climb up on the inside only, using the bars of the frames as handgrips and footholds. There are a sufficient number of these to make almost anyone feel as nimble as a monkey.

Never lean a ladder against a tower to reach the working platform either.

Some manufacturers make special clip-on ladders which are fixed inside the framework, making it far easier for the less agile to climb up or down.

At the working platform height, the various safety bars – hand and guard rails – can be fixed. The working platform boards then can be put in position.

Although the towers provide the safest way of working at height, the erection procedures must be followed closely to avoid the possibility of accidents.

If the tower is to be used on grass or other soft surface, a firm base must be laid to prevent the legs sinking in. A suitable base can be provided by laying down stout boards as bearers.

In all cases individual manufacturers' instructions and recommendations for use must be read and followed closely.

Moving a tower to a new work position is more convenient where castors are fitted – provided that the ground is even. It does not take a great deal of effort to push a tower along.

There are usually restrictions on how high a tower can be when castors are fitted. Incidentally, no one should even be allowed to remain on the tower during repositioning and no tools or equipment should be left on the platform. These could easily be dislodged and fall on your head.

Always make sure that the castors' locking device is in operation before scaling a tower.

Some towers can be pulled along on level ground without castors – but again there are manufacturers' height restrictions.

Once a tower reaches a certain height (specified in the instructions), it has to be tied to a building or other permanent support.

Apart from high towers for dealing with top windows, gutters and so on, other tower arrangements can be formed for dealing with interior ceilings and for similar purposes.

There are two ways of obtaining a tower. You can buy or you can hire one. In either case you must specify the number of frames you need and any accessories – castors, adjustable legs and so on, but if you buy, manufacturers will send a leaflet setting out the parts needed to build up a tower to various heights.

You only have to buy the amount you need. If you only want a low level job for interior work, you will not need many frames.

The components for towers are not cheap. However, if a group of people, club, association or neighbours get together the expenses could be shared.

A 16ft. tower is not likely to be needed very often by one person. It could be used only once a year which would mean it lying redundant the rest of the time. With a group scheme, much fuller use is assured.

On the other hand, as I mentioned earlier, the tower components are very versatile. You can use frames to make such things as a temporary workbench or kiddies climbing frame (at low level of course) when they are not being used for the tower.

Adding more frames.

Checking with a spirit level.

First frames positioned on adjustable bases. Note the timber base provided on the grass.

Adjusting a base.

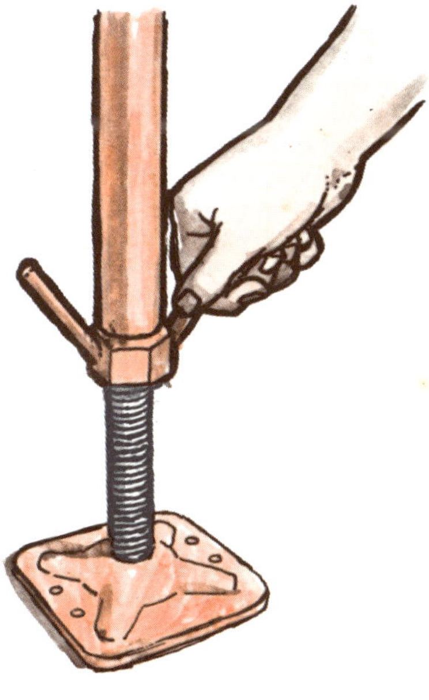

Using Man-made Boards

Hardboard, chipboard and plywood are names that nearly everyone has encountered. It is quite usual to hear someone recommending the use of chipboard 'to knock up some cupboards' or plywood 'to make some shelves' but unless you have had some practical experience there may be some uncertainty about buying and working with these materials.

Nowadays, with timber prices so high, these materials must be used for much that the handyman does.

Indeed there are many occasions where, by employing them, a much better end product will result, with far less work. So, let us take a close look at each of these man-made materials individually.

HARDBOARD

Hardboard is made from reconstructed wood fibres minus the bark and knots.

There are a dozen different types in the group, all serving specific purposes.

Standard hardboard can be used for a variety of jobs – for wall and ceiling panelling, covering uneven floors, panelling a softwood framework when making cupboards, fitted wardrobes and so on.

Medium grade hardboard can be used for the interior uses outlined above, though exterior grades are also available. They are thicker boards and therefore more rigid, but less dense than the standard type.

Hardboards with a melamine facing are called plastic-faced. Various colours and patterns are available, making them ideal for use in the kitchen for working surfaces and for splashbacks.

If you need to line the walls in the kitchen or bathroom, or enclose the bath behind panelling, you could use an enamelled board. Again, there is a whole range of colours from which to choose. There are also patterned and tile designs. Surface textures offered are gloss and matt.

If you like the idea of an embossed surface, then have a look at some moulded hardboards. There is a reasonable selection of pattern types available making them suitable for pelmets, panelling and other decorative uses.

For a woodgrain effect, choose hardboard with the prefix 'woodgrain'. There is a good choice of grain types. The obvious application for these is in furniture making.

Most of us have seen pegboard used in a variety of ingenious ways. Pegboard is hardboard covered with holes of various diameters – either uniform or irregular – and in various pattern arrangements.

Clips fit into the holes on which you can hang up kitchen utensils or tools so that they can be selected at a glance.

Insulating board is another hardboard type. This is a thermal insulating material with a wide range of decorative finishes. There are three types:

Fibre insulating boards are lightweight and porous to give a good heat insulation.

These come in plain, or textured surfaces and are available in the form of large sheets, planks or tiles.

Acoustic board is the second type, which will increase sound absorbtion. It is, in fact, a treated insulating board and comes in the form of tiles or board.

Should you wish to insulate and decorate at the same time, choose a third type – surfaced insulating boards. The surfaces are available in a wide range of materials – paper, textiles, sheet plastics, veneers.

The thickness and size of the sheets of hardboard varies with type. The types listed here vary in thickness between $\frac{1}{8}$in., $\frac{3}{16}$in., $\frac{1}{4}$in. and $\frac{1}{2}$in. Some are available in three of the sizes, others in only one.

All are sold in large sheets, 4ft. × 6ft. being the smallest size; 4ft. × 12ft. is the largest in some cases; in other types, moulded and plastic faced for examples, 4ft. × 8ft. is the maximum.

Insulating boards are thicker. The acoustic board is available only in two sizes – $\frac{1}{2}$in. and $\frac{3}{4}$in. The other types can be bought 1in. thick. Overall dimensions are basically the same as above. Tiles come in 1ft., 1ft. 4in. and 2ft. squares.

You can regard hardboard, more or less, as a piece of natural timber when it comes to working with it. Your normal woodworking tools will be suitable.

A couple of points to watch though, are that a fine tooth saw should be used to cut the standard types.

And, when dealing with a decorative faced board, it is always best to score along the intended saw line with a sharp knife. This avoids the possibility of the saw chipping the decorative surface. You will find that a rough edge is usually left after sawing. This can be cleaned off with glasspaper.

Earlier, when outlining the various ways that hardboard can be used, panelling over a softwood framework was mentioned. You can fix the hardboard with nails, screws or woodworking adhesive.

The method chosen depends on the job and is based on requirements such as the desired strength and appearance of the item.

Where standard hardboard is being used to cover a floor, fix it with hardboard pins. Adhesive can be used also if desired.

To avoid the standard board buckling in use, it must be conditioned, see page 31. Insulating boards and medium hardboards should be left standing on edge in the room where they are to be used for 48 hours before fixing. Do not stack the boards butted up to each other; keep them separated so that the air will flow around all surfaces freely.

Many people, in order to give the ground floor of their home an open plan look, remove one or more doors. The resultant gap – left as a rectangle – is hardly attractive. However, an arch can be built into the opening by bending hardboard to the appropriate shape and fitting it into the frame.

Various methods are used to bend hardboard. A large radius bend can be made by pinning one end of a standard sheet to a support framework and gradually working around to the other end of the sheet, pinning it to the framework as you proceed.

Hardboard can be finished with paint or sealer. The latter is especially suitable where the board is being used as a decorative surface covering over poor floorboards.

The surface of hardboard is smooth and tough, and will be further toughened and protected by applying a couple of coats of sealer. Wax polish provides additional protection.

If you choose a paint finish, start off with a coat of hardboard primer or emulsion diluted with water. If the hardboard is being used outside the home, start with a coat of aluminium-based primer.

After the priming coat, complete the job with normal undercoat and top coat.

CHIPBOARD

Chipboard is perhaps the most versatile of all the man-made boards. Its applications are so numerous that a use could be found for it in every part of the house. Most people use it for furniture making and, in fact, much of the factory produced furniture of today uses chipboard as its base.

The obvious advantage of making your own built-in furniture is that you do not have to compromise between what is available and what you want, at least as far as dimensions are concerned.

It is most irritating when you want to buy a fitted unit to slot neatly into a vacant alcove and you cannot find anything of the right dimensions, so you purchase the nearest possible size and learn to live with the ugly gaps that are left between the sides of the unit and the walls. This is never a satisfactory arrangement.

There are a great many types of chipboard available to perform different functions. There are surface finished grades that are prepared all ready for painting, boards with decorative surface finishes of plastic, wood veneer or metal, or melamine boards bonded to vinyl, textile covering on a paper backing, hessian and so on. There are also special fire-retardant and water resistant grades.

Chipboard is a homogeneous material with no grain. It is made from wood particles which, after being coated with a resin adhesive, are subjected to intense pressure and heat.

There are two main density types – the density of a board governs its strength – and these are called standard and flooring grade boards. The latter type is heavier. The standard type is used in furniture making and general building work.

Care must be taken to select the right grade of chipboard for particular purposes. Though it is sufficiently strong for most applications, it does not have the same strength as solid timber.

Good do-it-yourself shops and timber merchants will stock a selection of chipboard types. Certainly the standard grade will be readily available.

The standard board size is 8ft. × 4ft. in thicknesses of 18mm. ($\frac{3}{4}$in.) and 12mm. ($\frac{1}{2}$in.).

Proprietary brands of chipboard, such as Contiboard and Handiboard are readily available. These have decorative surfaces over a chipboard core.

Using a straight-edge to check that an edge of a chipboard sheet is even.

Working with chipboard is enjoyable since the boards are easy to cut and join. A unit of furniture, therefore, can be built relatively quickly.

The first essential is to take great care at the marking out stage. Always follow the golden rule 'mark twice and cut once'.

Do not assume that the edge of a sheet of chipboard is true or that corners are at right angles, important requirements if a finished item is to be square.

Use a straight-edge to ascertain if there are any bumps in the edge of the sheets. If there are, level them off with a plane. Once a true edge has been established, use this to take measurements from.

Your marking pencil should have a fine point – if the lead is thick it will give rise to inaccuracies. Even better than a pencil is a marking knife. Use a straight-edge to join up lines.

When you cut a length off a sheet it is unlikely that the saw will have left a true-cut edge, even though it appears to have followed the marked guide lines exactly. Always keep checking to ensure that an edge is true and corners are at right angles.

Incidentally, never fall into the trap of assuming that from a 4ft. wide sheet of any board (or natural timber) that you will be able to cut four pieces, each 1ft. wide. This is not so. You will end up with three pieces each 1ft. wide but the fourth piece will only be about 11$\frac{3}{4}$in. wide. The lost $\frac{1}{4}$in. is accounted for by the saw cuts.

The resin in chipboard tends to wear out saws more quickly than would natural timber. Should you have a tungsten carbide tipped general purpose saw in your kit, this is the ideal tool to use. If you work with hand tools, then use a fine tooth saw as this will produce a cleaner cut.

A couple of important points to note when using a power saw: the distance that the edge of the circular saw blade is above the board, determines the cleanness of the cut made.

Should the blade project too much – or too little – then the bottom or top surface of the board, respectively, will be chipped. The ideal projection is somewhere between $\frac{1}{8}$in. and $\frac{1}{4}$in. Should chipping still occur between these points, then increase the speed of the saw or reduce the rate at which the board is fed into the cutting blade.

Boards with a plastic laminate covering should be cut with a tungsten carbide tipped power saw. The brittle surface is less likely to be chipped if a slow rate of feed is used and a smaller diameter saw blade is fitted.

If the cut edges have to be planed smooth, then a normal hand plane or a Stanley Surform will do the trick.

Never plane the surface of chipboard.

Should you intend to cover the cut edge with an edge lipping material, then planing beforehand is advisable.

However, should you intend an edge to remain uncovered or painted, then it is preferable to finish by sanding the edges.

Depending on the degree of smoothness aimed at, use 120 to 200 grit grade sandpaper.

The points of the nails should project through the board.

Place the boards together and knock the nails home.

Jointing chipboard Provided that clean saw cuts are made, chipboard sections can be glued together very effectively. Liberally coat the mating edges with adhesive before positioning the sections in their correct positions. Clamps must be applied until the adhesive has set.

The adhesive to use is a pva type or a synthetic resin glue.

Where a piece of furniture or anything else is likely to have to withstand a lot of wear and tear, then a stronger joint should be made, using either nails or screws in addition to the adhesive.

When using nails, first knock them into one of the two boards to be joined. They should be in a straight line with their points just projecting through the other side of the board.

Apply glue to the mating edges according to manufacturer's instructions. Next, bring the two boards together in their correct position. Drive home the nails and apply clamps until the glue has set.

PLYWOOD

Plywood is constructed from various timbers including birch, pine and beech.

Veneers of these timbers are cut from the log and are joined together with the grain of each sheet running at right angles to the one below it. Resin adhesive is used to join the veneers.

Special adhesive grades are used dependent on whether the plywood is to be used for inside work (interior grade) or for outside work (exterior grade).

The layers of veneer are called plies; hence a board containing three plies is called three-ply, five plies are called five-ply; over this number the board is called multi-ply.

When buying plywood, the species, overall dimensions, thickness, grade and construction, must all be stated.

The species refers to the timber used. The overall dimensions are the length and the width – many sizes are available from 4ft. × 4ft. to 5ft. × 12ft. Thicknesses go from 3mm. to 25mm. The grade refers to whether it is for interior or exterior use. The construction means the number of plies.

The timber grade you use depends on the way that the plywood will be finished. Finnish birch plywood, for example, is available in various qualities – as are all the plywood types.

If a standard paint coat is to be used, then B quality should be specified. Should a high class paint finish, or staining, or clear sealing, be required then ask for BB quality.

There are other grades for lesser used finishing techniques which will not generally concern the average handyman.

There are no special problems to overcome when working with plywood. It can be cut, drilled, and shaped in much the same way as natural timber.

A clean cut will be made with a fine tooth saw. For shaped cuts, use the conventional bowsaw, padsaw, or fretsaw. If using power equipment, then a jigsaw or bandsaw will make a clean cut.

Plane inwards from the corners to the middle to avoid chipping the corners.

Thicker plywood will take a drill without fear of splitting the grain. Where the thinner grades are being used, use a backing of softwood.

Drill through the plywood into the softwood – a clean hole will be left on both sides of the plywood. If a backing material is not used, the drill could split the back of a thin sheet as it breaks through.

The only point to remember, when planing edges, is to work inwards from the corners to the middle. If you plane towards the corners, chipping could result at the corners themselves.

Sheets of plywood can be joined with glue or screws.

Plywood can be bent quite easily without having to condition the sheet as with hardboard. Use thin sheets only and bend them in the direction of the face grain. Should a thick curved panel be required, then use two or more thinner boards to achieve the desired thickness.

Putting Up Shelves

Every house needs shelves – lots of them. There are books, ornaments, glasses, chinaware, photographs and a hundred and one other things in most homes that need to be displayed or simply stored.

So the home handyman is faced with the age old job of putting up a shelf. It is a relatively simple task but then so are many other jobs – if you have the know-how.

The following stages are involved: selecting the materials and cutting them to size, drilling the wall to receive the fixing screws, fitting suitable wallplugs and, finally, fixing the shelf.

Obviously you can choose a proprietary shelving system – there are many available on the market – but this will still involve you in having to screw into the wall and will cost more.

For economy and freedom of design, it is preferable to make your own shelves from scratch, using softwood bearers to support a shelf of man-made material – chipboard or plywood.

The bearers have to be screwed to the wall, so the first thing to do is to make certain that it is safe to drill into the bricks, remembering that electric cables and plumbing pipes may be below the surface.

To drill a hole in the wall, you will need a drill – either hand or power operated – and a masonry drill bit. The bit fits into the chuck (the nose) of the drill. The bits come in various sizes, indicated by a number.

When the hole is drilled, a wallplug must be inserted to hold the screw.

The wallplug and the screw must be the same size as the masonry bit used. Thus, you would select, say, a No. 8 bit, a No. 8 drill and a No. 8 screw. The number eight refers to the diameter of the screw – not its length. Many diameters are available but for the purpose of fixing shelving bearers, a number eight is usually used.

No. 8 screws are made in various lengths; for shelf bearers, $1\frac{1}{2}$in. to 3in. will cover most needs. The length used is determined by the thickness of the bearers and the load that the shelf has to carry.

For example, a shelf intended to carry heavy kitchen pots and pans would need thick softwood bearers (say 2in. × 1in.) and long screws (say $2\frac{1}{2}$in. to 3in.). A display shelf intended for lightweight ornaments might have 1in. × $\frac{1}{2}$in. bearers fixed with $1\frac{1}{2}$in. long screws.

Brick walls are covered by a layer of plaster and this is not strong enough to hold a screw. The threaded part of the screw has to go right into the brickwork behind the plaster.

Since a screw will not grip on to brickwork, the wallplug has to be inserted into the pre-drilled hole.

Wallplugs come in two main materials – plastic and fibre, but as an alternative, many people prefer to use asbestos filling compounds in preference to wallplugs. These compounds have the advantage that they will fill a hole of any irregular shape and size. All you have to do is to moisten a little of the material with water, roll it into a plug and push it into the hole in the wall. Almost immediately, a screw can be inserted into the plug.

Incidentally, since the hole in the wall should be the same length as the screw to be inserted, you will have to know when to stop drilling into the wall. A good idea for, say a 3in. deep hole is to tie a piece of cotton to the drill bit at 3in. from its tip. When the cotton reaches the surface of the wall, the whole will be 3in. deep in the wall.

In modern houses, many internal walls are hollow. They are constructed of plasterboard fixed to a wood framework. Often the thickness of the plasterboard is only 10mm. Since their are no bricks behind it, a screw cannot be inserted.

For this situation, there are special cavity wall fixings.

SPRING TOGGLES These have 'wings' which open after being passed through a hole drilled in the plasterboard. The screw at the front is then tightened causing the wings to grip on to the back of the plasterboard. These devices can never be removed after fixing.

GRAVITY TOGGLES These have a hinged section which again is fed through a pre-drilled hole in the plasterboard. The hinged section drops down at right angles and grips the plasterboard at the back when the screw at the front is tightened. Thus the hinged section acts as an anchor. These devices cannot be removed.

RAWLNUTS Should an irregular size hole be drilled, these are useful. They have a rubber sleeve which expands as the screw is tightened and shapes itself to the contours of the

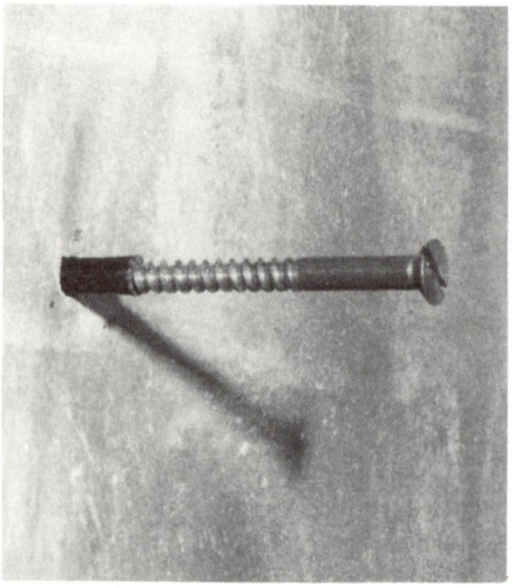

Rawlplug.

Rawlnut.

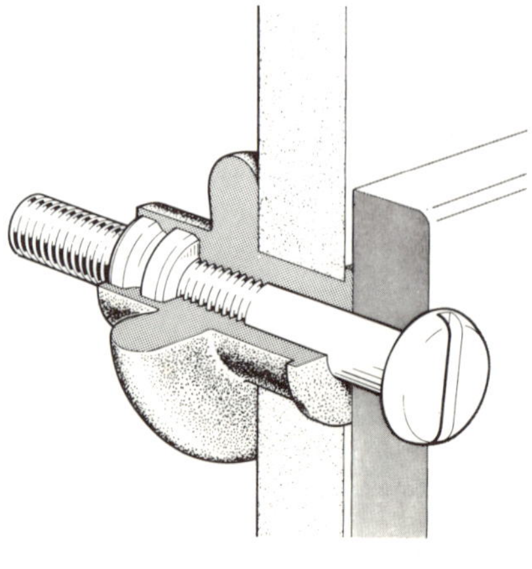

cavity. These can be removed and re-used.

RAWLANCHORS These have thick metal arms which spread out behind the plasterboard as the screw is tightened at the front.

FIXING A SHELF IN A RECESS

To make a shelf for a recess, you need two softwood bearers plus the shelf material (chipboard, plywood, etc.). The length of the bearers should be about $\frac{1}{2}$in. less than the depth of the shelf so that they will be set back from the front of the shelf and will not show.

Drill holes through the bearers at both the front and the back of each bearer.

Place one bearer in position on the wall using a spirit level to make sure it is horizontal. Use a pointed implement to transfer the hole positions on to the wall.

Drill the holes in the wall and insert the wallplugs and the screws to secure the bearer.

Use the spirit level again to draw a line across the recess on the line of the shelf to ensure that the second bearer is at the same level as the first one.

Fix the second bearer and then secure the shelf in place by screwing through it into the bearers.

For wide recesses or shelves to carry a heavy load, a long bearer should be screwed to the back wall between the two side bearers to support the centre of the shelf.

Marking screw holes through the first bearer.

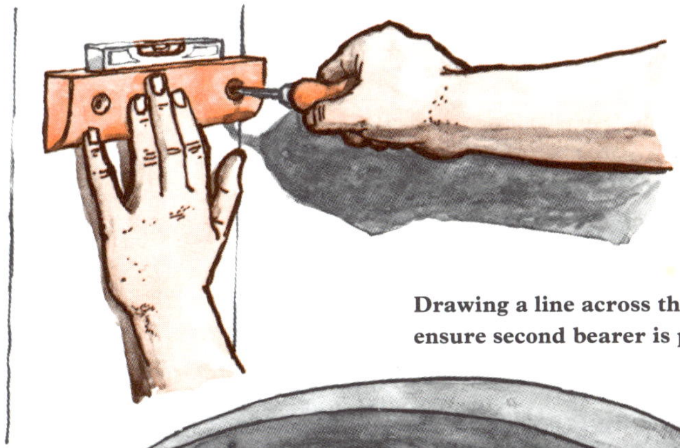

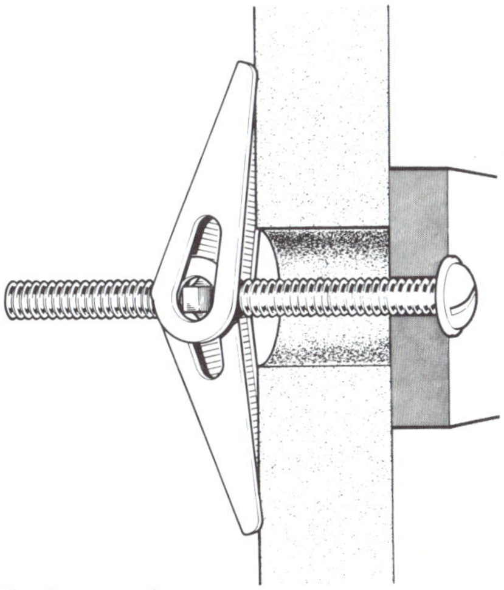

Spring toggle.

Gravity toggle.

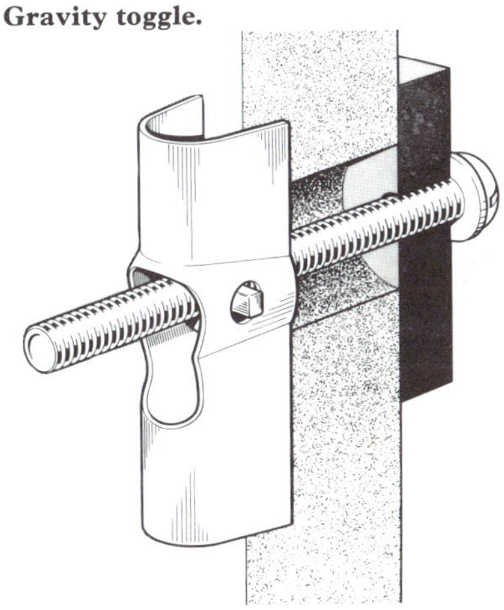

Drawing a line across the recess to ensure second bearer is parallel.

Index